Life With vvings

Recipes for Cooking and for Living

By

Ruth Baird Shaw

Cover & first page art by Derek McCrea

http://www.derekmccrea.50megs.com

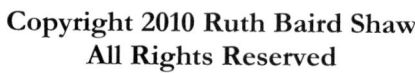

Life With Wings
By Ruth Baird Shaw
Third Edition
July 2010

ISBN 978-0-557-46759-4

90000

Note of Appreciation

This book is for my seven children, five sons-in-law and two daughters-in-law and present and future descendents of Charles and Ruth Shaw. This is also dedicated to my nephews and nieces and all descendents of my parents, Wilson and Ieula Baird, and of my parents-in-law, Grady and Lillian Shaw.

Ruth Shaw, 9th Grade Graduation

The first version of this book, ***Recipes, Rhymes and Reflections,*** was published in 1973 in response to suggestions by the Epworth United Methodist Women as an attraction for their bazaar. I still hear from people who have kept the little book. In 1998, Deborah Shaw Lewis reprinted the book to the delight of many.

My appreciation goes to the Rome Area Writers for help and encouragement in an expanded edition of ***Recipes, Rhymes & Reflections*** in 2003, put together quickly for a book signing sponsored by Friends of the Library. The expanded edition was designed and illustrated by the work and talent of my daughter, Beth Shaw Roszel.

A corrected and further expansion of the popular little book was made possible in 2008 by the editing and flawless English training of my daughter, Joan Shaw Turrentine, and the excellent work and professional editing and formatting of my daughter-in-law, Sheila Matthews Shaw.

I am indebted to Carol Shaw Johnston for her love, talent and expertise in this 2010 edition renamed ***Life With Wings*** and formatted for wider readership.

Although the poems and reflections are mine, it was a family affair to put them altogether into book form.

Poetry is meant to be spoken and homilies, by definition, are oral. Many of these poems were read in poetry programs in return invitations to church and civic groups. The homilies are the written form of oral presentations in Sunday worship.

Thanks to all those who shared their hospitality, their faith and their recipes in the churches where my husband, Rev. Charles Shaw, served: Dunkinsville, Cedar Mills and Jacksonville Methodist Circuit in Portsmouth, Ohio; Mackville and Antioch Methodist Circuit in Kentucky; Midway-Sunnyside-Vaughn in Griffin; Ellijay First Methodist; Trinity in Rome; Skyland, Epworth and Park Street Churches in Atlanta; Trinity in Austell; Forest Park First UMC; and Rico in Palmetto.

Special thanks also for the love, hospitality and cooperation of the people in the churches I served as pastor: Rico United Methodist Church in Palmetto, 1986-1990; Grantville First United Methodist, 1990-1993; and East Point Avenue United Methodist, 1993-1997. After retiring to Rome in 1997, I served on the staff at Trinity United Methodist until 2001, served as Interim Pastor at Oostanaula UMC for thirteen months, at Lyerly UMC for five months and Livingston United Methodist for twelve months.

~Ruth Baird Shaw, July 2010~

Table of Contents

Our Inheritance

C.S. Lewis is quoted as saying, "There is a profound democracy in creation. The deepest delights and the most enduring meaning come from the things we all inherit." God has taken action on behalf of each one of us. How tragic for us, then, to live joyless, miserable lives when we have been given the privilege of communication with God.

Silence is the drama
Of the day
When I alone with God,
Stop to pray.
I go into my closet
Of despair,
With burdens immovable
God is there!

My faith is a grain,
So mustard seed small
How can it be
That it has moved
My mountain of fear,
Into the sea?

~RBS~

Main Dishes

Ruth, Janice, and Charles

Chicken Mousse

1 large hen or two fryers
2 cups chicken stock (fat skimmed off)
2 cups mayonnaise
1 cup tiny English peas
1 cup blanched almonds (cut finely)
5 Tablespoons finely chopped pickles
1 envelope gelatin
4 hard cooked eggs (chopped finely)
1 small onion (grated)
1 cup finely chopped celery

Carol, Debi, Beth, David and Terry in front of the Ellijay, Georgia parsonage

Boil chicken in enough water to cover until well done. Discard skin and chop meat finely. (*This is an old recipe. One could substitute an equal amount of cooked boneless chicken and canned broth. In that case, do not skim off the little fat on top of the canned broth*). Dissolve gelatin in ¼ cup cold water. Add boiling stock. Add other ingredients and pour into oblong pan or mold. Refrigerate until firm. Cut into squares and serve. (*This is great for a women's luncheon dish, but I have also had men ask for this recipe many times*).

Stir-Fry Chicken

Boneless chicken
Fresh broccoli
carrots
cauliflower (optional)

soy sauce
corn starch
garlic powder
water chestnuts (optional)

Slice boneless chicken into large bite size pieces. Dredge in corn starch seasoned with garlic powder. Cook chicken pieces in fry pan or wok, stirring constantly in oil. Add soy sauce. Add fresh broccoli pieces and diagonally sliced carrots. Sprinkle with soy sauce and continue stirring until vegetables are slightly cooked. Cauliflower and water chestnuts may be added. Do not overcook. Serve with rice.

Chicken Loaf

1 hen (or two fryers)
1 small carrot
2 stalks celery
1 small onion
1 cup cooked rice
1 ½ cups bread crumbs
1 tsp. salt
5 eggs (beaten)
3 cups chicken broth (fat skimmed off)

Place chicken in large vessel with carrot, celery, onion and salt. Cover with water and cook until tender.

Let chicken cook in stock. When cold, drain, saving stock. Discard skin, bones and onion. Dice chicken, carrot and celery and combine with other ingredients. *(I usually add a little black pepper and about ¼ tsp. sage and a little more salt, if needed).*

Place in greased baking dish. Mixture will be thin but will firm up in baking.) Bake about 1 ½ hours at 350 degrees. Place foil on top if it begins to get too brown. Cut into squares to serve with mushroom sauce. Serves about 12 to 15 people generously.

Charles

Mushroom Sauce

¼ cup flour
1 tsp. chopped parsley
1 can cream of mushroom soup
1 tsp. lemon juice
1 egg yolks, beaten

Mix well and cook over low heat until thick. *(I always add the two extra egg whites to the loaf).*

Chicken Almandine

Chicken pieces (chicken tenders
can be used with great success)
1 tsp. salt
1 tsp. paprika
¼ tsp. pepper
1/3 cup margarine
1 cup orange juice
1/3 cup blanched almonds
(toasted and chopped)

Rub combined seasonings into
chicken and sauté in the
margarine until golden brown on
both sides. Cover pan and cook
slowly until chicken is tender:
25-30 minutes. Remove from pan
and keep warm. Pour orange juice
into pan. Stir to loosen any brown
particles and cook until boiled down
to one half. Thicken with 1 tsp.
cornstarch and 1 tsp. water. Pour
sauce over chicken pieces and sprinkle
with the chopped almonds.

*Charles snapped this shot of the family on
vacation in Florida. (l-r) Beth, Janice,
Joan, Carol, Terry, Debi and Ruth*

Lasagna

1 lb. lean ground beef
1 small onion, grated
½ tsp. oregano
½ tsp. garlic salt
1 lb. grated cheese

Lasagna noodles (8 pieces, cooked)
1 can tomato paste
1 can tomato soup
1 tsp. salt
¾ tsp. pepper

Brown meat. Add seasoning and tomato soup and paste with about ½ can water.
Simmer meat sauce about 30 minutes. Layer in ungreased baking dish: First, a
thin layer of sauce, then the noodles, then a layer of meat sauce. Cover top with
cheese or slices of cheese. Bake in 325 oven until cheese has melted.

Ruth and Terry

Instant Brunswick Stew

2 cans barbeque pork (10 oz. cans)
2 cans barbeque beef (10 oz. cans)
2 cans boned chicken (13 oz. cans)
2 cans crushed tomatoes (28 oz. cans)
2 cans cream style corn (16 oz. cans)

Combine all and heat thoroughly and serve.
(For those of us who have made Brunswick stew the old fashioned way, we know it to be a four-letter word called "work.")

"Zero Points" Soup

5-ounce pkg. fresh baby spinach, chopped
10-ounce pkg. grated carrots
2 28-ounce cans diced tomatoes
2 quarts vegetable broth
1 large onion, diced
1 clove garlic, diced

2 stalks celery, diced
1 bell pepper, diced
1 Tablespoon dried basil
1 teaspoon dried oregano
Red pepper flakes (1/4 tsp – 2 tsp, depending on how spicy you like it)

Dump all the ingredients in a large soup pot, bring to a boil and simmer until the vegetables are tender. Season to taste with salt and pepper and enjoy. This makes a very large pot of soup. It's a great vegetarian dish. *(This soup got its name because on the Weight Watchers program, a serving is zero points.)*

Corn Bread Casserole

1 ½ lb. lean ground beef
1 small onion, chopped
1 can tomato sauce
3 oz. can mushrooms
1 tsp. salt
Pepper to taste

Cook beef and onions in skillet until lightly browned. Add tomato sauce, mushrooms, salt and pepper. Pour into a 2 qt. casserole and cover with cornbread batter. Bake at 450 degrees for 20 minutes.

Chili Soup

2 lbs. lean ground beef
1 large can tomatoes
4 medium sized potatoes (diced fine)
2 large onions (chopped fine)
4 tbsp. chili powder (more or less to taste)
2 or 3 cans beans (pinto, great northern, orpork and beans)
1 tsp. salt

Brown meat over low heat. Blend chopped onions and a can of tomatoes in blender and add to browned meat. Add diced potatoes. Simmer together about 1 hour. Add 2 or 3 cans of beans (*I usually add a can of pork and beans and a can or two of either pinto or great northern*). Simmer a few minutes more. Serve with corn muffins or saltines.

Chicken & Potato Soup

1 large fryer or chicken pieces
2 large onions
5 large potatoes
Salt and pepper to taste

Cook chicken in water until tender. Remove bones and skin, chop finely and set aside. Run onions and potatoes through blender and add to chicken broth to thicken.

(I use potatoes instead of flour for flavor and to thicken the soup. If not thick enough, flour can be added to the desired consistency. If broth is not rich enough, add a can or 2 of chicken broth or cream of chicken soup. This makes 5 or 6 quarts of delicious soup).

Beth and Ruth

An Ode to Daughters

I wrote "An Ode to Daughters" for the annual UMW Mother-Daughter Banquet at Trinity Austell UMC at the request of the chair of programs.

This is for our five daughters: Janice Dianne, Lynda Joan, Mary Carol, Deborah Ruth and Sharlyn Beth and our daughters-in-law: Sheila Ann and Vicki Elaine.

This poem honors our granddaughters: Sharon Lyn, Laura Charmaine, Larisa Carron, Amanda Ruth, Brannon Ruth, Sarah Lisette, Jessica Ruthanne, Lillian Matthews, Catherine Nicole, Haley Elizabeth, and granddaughters-in-law: Naomi Louise, La Donna Elizabeth, Meleah Elaine, Emily Marie and Michaela.

This is also for our great-granddaughters: Rachael Elizabeth, Hannah Ruth, Helena Gilbert, Stefani Brianne, AnnaGrace Catherine, Natalie Joan, Sarah Shaw Carr, Lillian Sarah, Sophia Vaughn, Emma Lynn and Evelyn Ann – with love and prayers from Grandma Ruth.

Joan   *Sheila*

Janice   *Carol*

Beth

Debi   *Vicki*

An Ode to Daughters

An ode to our daughters
A "word bouquet"
How can I find
Words to convey…

The worth of a daughter?
The question asked
My mind could never
Meet the task.

My mind consulted
With my heart
And right away
Knew where to start.

Start at the beginning
When each baby girl
Was a dream in the heart
Of an unborn world!

"It's a girl," a wee baby
Just perfect . . . a girl!
I envisioned white ruffles
In a pink ribboned world.

She's a girl . . . in pink softness
And colors . . . like these . . .
Red measles, yellow jaundice
And black and blue knees!

She's a girl . . . she is growing.
She is trying her wings,
Dear Lord, keep her safe
From life's hurts and stings.

She's a girl! She's a treasure . . .
That I recommend!
For she's always a daughter,
And more. She's a friend!

~RBS~

Janice   *Joan*   *Beth, Ruth, Debi and Carol*

When I was asked to write a poem for our 1976 Atlanta - College Park District United Methodist Pastors' Valentine Banquet program, I came up with a poem that is a favorite of my children. The poem is a fun piece about married love and is full of clichés and inside jokes for pastors. I hope it adds to the charm of the poem.

We

I was I and he was he
A ceremony made us "we."
When in the sight of God and men
We pledged our troth and kissed our kin
And set our sails ... breathlessly
On the matrimony sea.

My handsome prince. . . he held my hand.
My every wish. . . was his command
Until one day. . . I said, "I think we
Should see my friends. . . more frequently.

He said, so loud ... it shook the house
That he was man ... and not a mouse
And furthermore ... he said we should
See his friends ... he said we would.

He said, we would ... most certainly
I said, we won't ... we both said "we"
Strange, when we do ... or don't agree
One thing is clear ... we both say "we"

Now that's the secret ... for love to grow
Through Summer's sun ... and Winter's snow
Through diaper rash ... and teething ills
From P.T.A. ... to college bills

Through three-point charge ... and inner-city
And Pastor Parish Relations Committee
Through Conference moving time ... again
When you're not one ... of the bishop's men.

Through covered dishes ... well, thick and thin
Love like this ... will never end
For when we do ... or don't agree
We still find joy ... in being "we".

~RBS, February 1976~

A Woman's Work Is Never Done

In oral presentations of this poem I usually introduce it with two stories. One of the stories is about newlyweds. One day the bride told her husband that the Bible stated that men were to do the dishes. He was aghast! She got out the Bible and read: 2 Kings 21:13: "I will stretch over Jerusalem the line of Samaria, and the plummet of the house of Ahab. And I will wipe Jerusalem as a man wipeth a dish, wiping it and turning it upside down."

The second story has three women out riding. An accident rushes all three to the entrance to the "pearly gates" and Saint Peter. The Catholic lady showed St. Peter her well-used rosary. The Baptist lady had a well-marked Bible to show her Christian dedication. The Methodist woman kept digging into her large purse saying, "I know there is a covered dish in here somewhere."

This poem, like several others, was written "tongue in cheek" and while I was the busy mother of small children.

l-r: Joan holding doll, Charles holding Terry and Carol,
Ruth holding Debi, and Janice

A Woman's Work Is Never Done

That poem that came ... into my heart
Unexpected ... like a dart
I want to polish ... for discerning
To write it down ... oh, the yearning.

First, I must polish ... something more
That spot from off ... the kitchen floor.
What did I write? ... a note that said,
"Excuse my child ... he's sick in bed."

I also write ... some words to note:
Call the dentist ... hem brown coat,
Wash blue sweater ... start the roast,
Toss a salad ... buy bread for toast.

Wash the dishes ... fold the clothes,
Sew a blouse ... buy ribbon bows,
Make a poster ... draw a fish,
Prepare another ... covered dish.

Wash the windows ... doors and sill,
Grab the telephone ... pay the bills.
Buy quick oatmeal ... cream of wheat,
Call repair man ... mend a sheet.

Set the table ... kiss a hurt,
Iron a tablecloth ... blouse and skirt,
And other chores ... I list and do.
Just little things ... the whole day through

So I continue ... blowing noses
And postpone things ... like Grandma Moses.
But thank you, God ... You did your part,
You placed a poem ... within my heart.

~RBS~

A Letter from Camp

David, our youngest, reached age 11 and was excited to take his place for a week at Camp Glisson in Dahlonega, the family tradition his six siblings before him had enjoyed.

As his mother, I helped him pack for the trip. I had bought new underwear for him and included the new package of underwear in his luggage. I also added a self-addressed card to send to us from camp as a good exercise in writing.

Fortunately David was back home with his head still attached and still "filling good" before the card below arrived.

Also ... his new underwear was still in the unopened package.

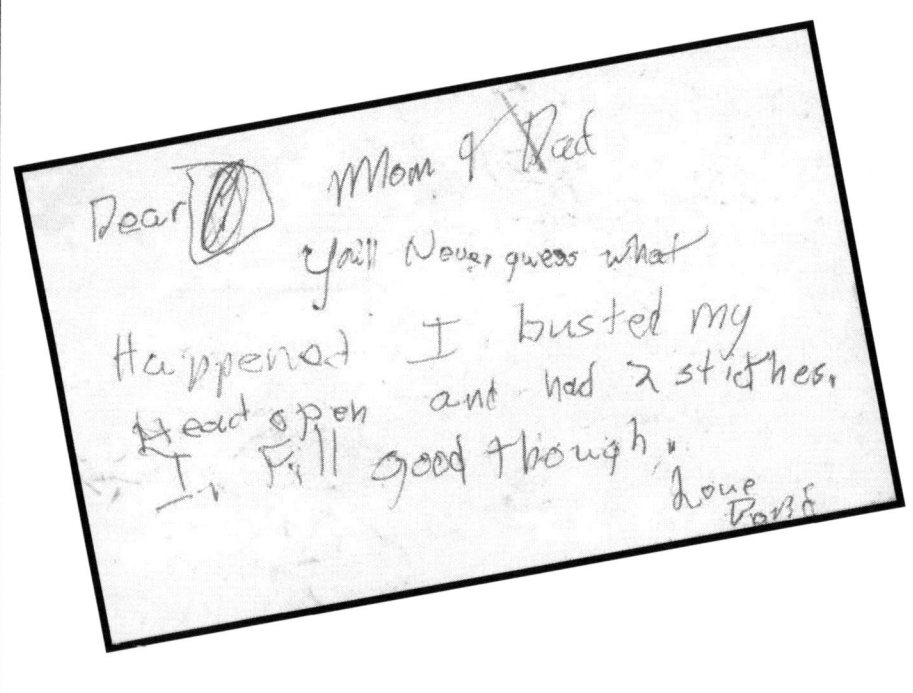

Vegetables
& Salads

back: Ruth and Charles, middle: Janice and Joan,
front: Terry and Carol

Green Bean Salad

1 can small whole green beans
1 can yellow wax beans
1 can red kidney beans

½ cup chopped green pepper
¼ cup finely chopped celery
1 white onion sliced very thin

Combine:
¾ cup sugar
½ cup vinegar
½ cup cooking oil

1 tsp. salt
½ tsp. pepper

Pour over drained vegetables and toss well. Refrigerate overnight.

Joan's Company Salad

1 head lettuce
1 onion (sliced very thinly)
1 bell pepper (chopped finely)
1 No. 2 can tiny English peas
2 cups mayonnaise

1 cup grated
parmesan
cheese

Place vegetables in layers beginning with the lettuce. Place peas on top. Cover with mayonnaise. Sprinkle cheese on top. Cover tightly and place in refrigerator overnight. The beauty of this salad is that it can be made a day or two before serving. It stays crisp and delicious.

Joan holding pet rabbit, raised for food but never eaten.

Oven Rice

1 cup rice
1 tbsp. salt

1 stick margarine
1 tbsp. vinegar

Put 3 cups hot water in oblong baking dish. Add other ingredients. Cover with foil and place in oven at 350 degrees for about 1 hour. When done, each grain of rice will stand apart.

Ruth's Squash Soufflé

2 cups squash, cooked and mashed
1 cup dry bread crumbs
1 cup milk
1 tbsp. grated onion
3 tbsp. bacon drippings or butter
2 eggs beaten
salt and pepper to taste

Mix all together, pour into a baking dish and
bake 20 to 30 minutes in 350 degree oven.

Beth and Terry

Sweet Potato Casserole

3 cups mashed sweet potatoes
½ cup sugar

¼ cup butter
2 eggs
1 tsp. vanilla

Combine and pour into baking dish. Top with:
1 cup coconut
1 cup chopped nuts
¾ cup brown sugar

¼ cup flour
¼ cup melted butter

Sprinkle over potatoes. Bake at 375 degrees for 30 minutes.

Marinated Carrots

2 lbs carrots (sliced)
1 small green pepper
1 medium onion
1 can tomato soup
½ cup oil

½ cup vinegar
¾ cup sugar
1 tsp. Worcestershire sauce
1 tsp. prepared mustard

Boil carrots in salted water until tender. Set aside and drain. Cut green pepper
and onions into rings or chop. Combine soup, oil, vinegar and seasonings and
heat until well blended. Pour over vegetables and refrigerate. *(This keeps well for
days).*

Lime Gelatin Salad

1 pkg. lime gelatin
1 cup boiling water
½ cup evaporated milk
1 cup crushed pineapple

1 tbsp. lemon juice
½ cup chopped nuts,
¼ tsp. salt
½ cup cottage cheese

Dissolve gelatin in boiling water and chill until partly set. Add remaining ingredients. Stir together and chill until firm.

Cucumber Sandwiches

1 pkg. (3oz.) cream cheese
1 medium cucumber, peeled, grated and drained
1 tsp. grated onion
Salt and while pepper to taste
Green food coloring (optional)
Bread slices

Combined all ingredients for filling and stir until smooth. Spread on thin slices of bread and cut into desired shapes. (*I usually cut the bread slices into circles before spreading filling on them.*) Yields 3/4 cup filling.

Ruth, Carol, Joan and Janice

Debi, Carol holding David, and Beth

Carol's Romaine-Strawberry-Walnut Salad

Ruth and Carol

1 head romaine lettuce
Fresh strawberries, sliced
Walnuts, chopped
Grated cheese (mixture of white
and yellow cheeses makes the
salad look nice)
Dressing (recipe below)

Wash and tear the lettuce into a
large salad bowl. Add the sliced
strawberries, chopped walnuts,
and grated cheese. Immediately before
serving, toss with the salad dressing.
*(This is a fabulous salad that has always drawn favorable comments whenever I've made it.
You can substitute mandarin orange segments and sliced almonds for the strawberries and
walnuts.)*

Dressing
¾ cup oil
¾ cup sugar
½ cup red wine vinegar
1 clove or 1 tsp. garlic

½ tsp. paprika
½ tsp. salt
¼ tsp. black pepper

Put ingredients in a blender and blend thoroughly. Shake well before tossing
with salad.

Quick Cranberry Salad

2 pkgs. raspberry gelatin
1½ cup hot water
1 can whole cranberry sauce
1 large can crushed pineapple
1 cup chopped pecans

Dissolve gelatin in hot water. Add cranberry sauce and mix well. Add pineapple
and nuts and refrigerate until firm. Serves 12.

Blue Cheese Dressing

1 pint mayonnaise
½ cup buttermilk
3 oz. blue cheese

½ tsp. pepper
½ tsp. celery salt

Mix well and refrigerate.

French Dressing

1 can tomato soup
1 tsp. prepared mustard
¼ cup sugar
½ cup vinegar

1 tsp. garlic
½ cup salad oil
1 tsp. salt
1 tsp. pepper

Mix in mixer or blender and refrigerate in covered jar.

Hollandaise Sauce

4 tbsp. sour cream
½ tsp. salt
2 tbsp. water
2 beaten egg yolks
1 tablespoon lemon juice

Combine and cook in double boiler until thick, making sure that the boiling water doesn't touch the pan. Serve over asparagus, broccoli, or Brussels sprouts.

The Light

A few years before my husband died, we bought a cemetery lot in East View in Conyers where his father and grandparents were buried. Charles was still in a busy pastorate, but late one afternoon we finally went down to see the lot and to visit his mother who lived nearby. As it began to get dark in the cemetery, I noticed lights going on in the homes near the cemetery. It seemed like a parable to me, comparable to parents leaving lights on at night for their children. And I wrote:

My father always left a light for me ...
Against the nighttime shadows ...
Lovingly.
He left the door unlocked ...

It opened wide
And I could safely find,
My way inside.

Beyond the grave
I see a light ... I see
The Lights of home.

God left a light for me.
So I can walk through death.
With faith ... not fear.
I see the lights of home,
And God is near!

~RBS, 1980~

The Lord is the light of my salvation; whom shall I fear? The Lord is the stronghold of my life; of whom shall I be afraid? ~Psalms 27:1~

Life with Wings

God created an artistic world. The arts, music, visual arts, paintings, drama, poetry are all embedded in our humanity. God over-created our world. He could have created in monochrome with no colorful flowers or sunsets. All food could have been tasteless manna. All birds could have been silent. Instead we have a world lavished with color and taste and sound and music.

I like the story Cecil B. DeMille told of being in a canoe in Maine one summer day. He was just drifting through the water in a shallow place near the shore. He could see the bottom of the lake and noticed it was covered with water beetles. One of the water beetles crawled up on a canoe, fastened its feet in the gunnels and died.

Three hours later, still floating in the warm sun, DeMille said he witnessed a miracle. The shell of the water beetle cracked open and a tiny head emerged. The wings unfolded and finally a beautiful dragonfly with iridescent body and gossamer wings left the dead carcass and sailed across the surface of the water, shimmering in the afternoon sun . . . going further in a half second than the water beetle could crawl all day long. The dragonfly sailed across the surface of the lake. But the water beetles below, unaware of the miracle of metamorphosis, could not see it.

DeMille said, "Do you think God would do that for a water beetle and not do it for you and me?"

Have you ever known the feeling of being lifted above ordinary limitations? Not just doing the best you can "under the circumstances" but allowing God to get you out from under the circumstances that would hold you?

I sat with a congregation listening to Charles Shaw, my pastor and husband, give a sermon. He told about an imaginary conversation someone had with an ordinary looking worm crawling down the road of a busy city. The worm was "out of place" but told the man, "Don't stop me. I'm going to get my wings." This is the poem I wrote as I listened to the sermon titled "Life with Wings."

Life with Wings

God made the butterfly
and I
stand on earth
and watch it fly.
And see that God
has fashioned wings
for even earthbound,
creeping things.

I know that God
intended wings
for you
and me
Oh, my heart sings.
I've found my wings
and even I
can over circumstances
fly!

~RBS~

The Old Woman in My Future

I have been somewhat out of step all my life. I started to school at five, skipped a grade and was the youngest in my class in elementary and high school, I married my childhood sweetheart, and we raised seven children. I went back to school after my children were grown. I suppose I aged into the study of aging. When I received my degree in Gerontology from Georgia State, one of my sons-in-law asked what I had learned about the subject of aging. I told him I had learned three things:

Old age is not a disease.

Ruth receiving degree at Georgia State University

We have to admit we do have more aches and pains and illnesses as we age, but age itself is not a disease. Willard Scott has written a book, *The Older the Fiddle, The Better the Tune*, which is the thesis of my *Autumn Wisdom* poem. A good illustration of this: An eighty-five-year-old lady went to the doctor with an excruciating pain in her left arm. The doctor could not find the problem so he finally told the lady, "I suppose it is just old age." She said, "Don't hand me that, doctor. My right arm is just as old as my left arm, and it is not hurting."

"Old" is not a dirty word.

There may be more discrimination against the aged than any other group. For example, when an older person has an accident - the same kind that happens to younger people every day - it is immediately assumed it is because they are too old to drive. Age has little to do with whether or not we can drive a car. However, health and other things associated with aging do matter. So we should not be like the man who said, "I can't see and I can't hear but thank God I can still drive!"

We are indeed living in a society that places great value on youth and at a time when "age" is often neither valued nor respected.

Old age is not a joke.

I often hear this statement while visiting the elderly. More jokes are written about old age than perhaps any other group. I have collected quite a few. There is a minister in a Presbyterian Church in Sandy Springs who has "The Ministry of Laughter." He contends that laughter is therapeutic and hastens physical healing. I have also read that laughter burns calories. Laughter keeps us in shape in more ways than one. A good sense of humor and especially the ability to laugh at oneself is necessary for us to enjoy life in old age as well as in youth.

I frequently get emails with amusing stories about the elderly. Here's a sampling:

A lady was taking her four-year-old daughter with her as she delivered Meals on Wheels. The little girl was intrigued and always asked questions about the various things she saw in the homes of the elderly - wheel chairs, canes, walkers. The mother found her little daughter staring at a pair of false teeth soaking in a glass and braced herself for the questions. The little girl, however, just turned to her mother and whispered, "The tooth fairy will never believe this."

One story Charles Swindoll tells in his book *Laugh Again* has to do with a grandmother spending the evening with her seven-year-old granddaughter. The little girl kept asking her grandmother her age. But the grandmother said, "Honey, I never tell anyone my age." She went to answer the phone and came back to find the little girl looking at her driver's license. The little girl said, "Grandmother I know how old you are. You are 69! And I know something else about you, Grandmother; you failed sex. It says right here, 'SEX- F.'"

I remember when I was a student at Georgia State, I was writing a paper about "The Senior Citizen Growing Older" and I sat there looking at what I had typed and realized that "growing older" is two words - not just one word, and one of the words is a positive word. "Growing" is a word that opens up all kinds of positive possibilities.

To some degree, at least, we can choose to **grow** old rather than just to **get** old. I did an internship in Gerontology at the Christian City Complex which included a nursing home, assisted living, Alzheimer's unit and retirees' homes. I saw examples of both kinds of aging. Some grew as they aged. Others just got old in fear and bitterness. It is true that often, when we walk into a nursing home and see the blank stares and the pitiful conditions of many, we say in our hearts, "O Lord, I don't want to get that old." And "old" seems to be tragic in many respects. However, statistics tell us that most of the elderly live in their own homes and have pretty good lives. The percentage of the frail, disabled elderly is small, much less than 10% the last time I checked.

But even so, regardless of our present age, if we live long enough, there is an old man or an old woman in our future.

The Old Woman in My Future

Regardless of our present age, if we live long enough there is an old man or an old woman in our future:

Someday ... Somehow ... Somewhere in time
She's waiting ... I will see
The old woman ... Time is making
Time is making ... out of me!

Will she be a sad complainer,
A fretful tenant of the earth?
Or a kind, productive person
Filled with happiness and mirth?

Please be patient ... God is making
Molding slowly ... Out of me
A shining portrait ... He has promised.
Just you wait and see.

He is smoothing out the roughness
Polishing the dreary places
Filling life with joy and gladness
Pouring out His gifts and graces.

God remake me ... in Your image.
I want to like her ... when I see
That old woman ... time is making,
Time is making ... out of me!

~RBS, 1984~

Breads & Beverages

*Charles Shaw, at one of many
covered dish luncheons*

Breakfast Muffins

1 egg
1 cup milk
2 tbsp. sugar
2 tbsp. melted shortening

2 cups sifted self-rising flour
½ cup chopped nuts or 1 cup blueberries

Beat egg. Add milk, shortening and sugar. Add to flour. Stir only until moistened. Add nuts or blueberries. Fill greased muffin cups 2/3 full. Bake in hot oven (400 degrees) until lightly browned.

Dora's Cheese Wafers

8 oz. sharp cheese grated
1 stick butter
1 cup flour
¼ tsp. red pepper
½ tsp. salt
2 cups crispy rice cereal

Mix well and make small balls. Place on cookie sheet and flatten with fork. Bake at 300 degrees. Wafers are done when they are brown around the edges.

Sausage Balls

1 lb. sausage
2 cups Bisquick
¾ lbs. sharp grated cheese

Mix together and knead well. Pinch off into tiny balls. Chill. Bake about 15 minutes at 350 degrees. Makes about 90 balls.

Mama Baird (Ieula Baird) with some of her grandchildren

Mama's Biscuits

Self-rising flour
Shortening
Buttermilk

Pin back your hair. Roll up your sleeves. Clean your fingernails. Wash your hands as if you were scrubbing for surgery. In a large bowl (preferably a wooden bowl), sift self-rising flour into the bowl about half full. With one clean hand, make a fist-size indentation in the flour. In the indentation put a large handful of shortening. Pour buttermilk, a little at a time, over the shortening and work in the flour. You are mixing the flour, shortening and milk together into a soft dough that you can handle and pinch off, roll around in your hands into golf size balls and flatten into biscuits onto a greased baking sheet.

Bake at 375 degrees until golden brown.

(The secret of good biscuits is to handle the dough as little as possible. With practice, one can make a large pan of beautiful biscuits the same size. Or the dough can be rolled out and cut with a biscuit cutter).

If you insist on mixing with a spoon, for a large pan of biscuits use about:

5 cups self-rising flour
2 cups shortening
2½ cups buttermilk

Mix flour and shortening together; stir in buttermilk. Mix together into a dough. Put dough on floured surface, roll out and cut with biscuit cutter. Place biscuits on greased baking pan. Bake at 375 degrees until golden brown.

Angel Biscuits

5 cups self-rising flour
1 cup shortening
¾ cup sugar
2 cups buttermilk

1 tsp. baking soda
3 pkgs. yeast (dissolved in 1/4 cup warm water)

Combine dry ingredients. Cut in shortening. Stir in yeast and buttermilk. Roll out and cut as desired and bake in hot oven (400 degrees). Dough may be covered tightly and kept in refrigerator for several weeks.

Perfect Rolls

2 pkgs. yeast
2 tsp. salt
½ cup sugar
½ cup shortening
½ cup dry skim milk powder
2 eggs
7 cups flour

Soften yeast in ½ cup warm water and stir until dissolved. In a large bowl, put salt, sugar and shortening. Add 2 cups hot water and stir until shortening is melted. Add dry milk powder. When mixture is lukewarm, stir in well beaten eggs and the yeast.

Ruth taking an afternoon break

Beat in about one-half of the sifted flour and beat well. Add the rest of the flour and knead on lightly floured surface for 15 minutes.

Put dough into a greased bowl. Cover with a damp cloth. Set in warm (not hot) place and let rise until double in bulk (about 1½ hours). Punch down. Let rise again until about double in bulk, approximately 40 minutes. Shape into rolls. Cover with a damp cloth and let rise until double in bulk, about one hour. Bake at 400 degrees until golden brown.

Coffee Cake

David reading by lantern light after an ice storm in Ellijay

Use the previous recipe for "Perfect Rolls" for this coffee cake. When the dough is ready to shape into rolls, divide the dough into three parts. On a lightly floured surface, roll each part into a rectangular shape (about 12 x 24 in.) Spread with softened margarine and sprinkle with sugar. (Add cinnamon and/or nuts, if desired). Roll up like a jelly roll. Slice into rolls about 1 inch thick. Arrange in pans. Cover with damp cloth and let rise until double in bulk.

Bake until lightly browned in 400 degree oven. While still warm, brush rolls with a thin glaze and sprinkle with nuts.

Coffee Cake Glaze

1 stick margarine
1 box confectioners' sugar
1 tsp. vanilla
Enough evaporated milk to make a thin icing

Combine all ingredients in a sauce pan. Keep warm and brush on rolls with a pastry brush.

Tiny Tea Rolls

To shape the rolls, pinch off enough dough to roll a strip about 20 inches by 4 inches wide by 1/8 inch thick. Roll on floured surface, spread with melted butter and sprinkle with sugar and cinnamon. Roll up so that you have a roll 20 inches long. Generously grease tiny muffin tins. Place ½ tsp. glaze (recipe on next page) in bottom of each. Slice the rolls 1 inch thick and place in muffin cups. Cover with cloth and let rise until double in bulk. Bake at 400 degrees for 10 to 12 minutes or until golden brown. Remove from oven and invert immediately on baking sheet. Lift off muffin tins, letting glaze run down over the rolls.

Tea Roll Glaze

Mix:
2 cups light brown sugar
½ cup soft margarine
5 tbsp. light corn syrup

Corn Bread Dressing

2½ cups crumbled corn bread
1 cup dry bread crumbs
4 cups chicken stock
½ cup drippings or margarine
1 small onion, chopped finely
2 stalks celery, chopped finely
1 tsp. salt
1 tsp. ground sage
¼ tsp. pepper
4 eggs slightly beaten

Combine ingredients. Add a little more
broth or water if needed to make mixture
thin. Bake 30 minutes at 400 degrees.

Janice and Joan

Giblet Gravy

Cook turkey or chicken neck and giblets in enough water to cover, until tender.
Chop meat finely. Set aside. Blend together:

3 heaping tbsp. flour
4 tbsp. drippings
4 cups broth from giblets

Cook until thick, stirring constantly. Add 1 tsp. Worcestershire sauce. Add salt
and pepper to taste. Add the chopped giblets. Serve with turkey and dressing.

Mamaw Turrentine's Boiled Custard

1 gallon whole milk
2½ cups sugar
6 large (or 7 medium) eggs
2 tsp. vanilla
1 heaping tbsp. plain flour (mixed with sugar)
Dash nutmeg (or cinnamon)

Keep back a cup of the milk. Bring rest of milk to a steam in top of a double boiler. (*I use a stock pot set inside a larger stock pot.*) Meanwhile, blend the cup of milk and eggs thoroughly in the blender. Add the sugar & flour to this mixture and mix briefly. Slowly stir the egg mixture into the steaming milk. Cook, stirring constantly, until

Terry and Debi

the custard thickens — quite a while. Fill sink with ice cubes, and set pot of cooked custard into sink. Stir the custard while it cools. This keeps it from curdling. Add vanilla and spice after the custard is cool. (*I sometimes add a few drops of yellow food coloring for aesthetic appeal.*)

Christmas Party Punch

1 6-oz. can frozen orange juice (defrosted)
1 6-oz. can frozen lemonade (defrosted)
2½ cups pineapple juice
1½ qt. cranberry juice

Add water to orange juice and lemonade according to directions on package. Pour all ingredients into punch bowl. Add ice mold. Serves 50.

Janice

Lime Economy Punch

6 pkgs. lemon-lime Kool-Aid
4 cans water
1 large can pineapple juice
5 cups sugar
1 large bottle ginger ale (add when ready to serve)

(I often substitute frozen lime or lemon juice for the pineapple juice. I have made this punch for children's parties, for Christmas teas, and for wedding receptions and have been asked for this recipe many times.)

Instant Russian Tea

1½ cups Tang
1½ cups sugar
1 cup lemon-flavored instant tea
1 tsp. cinnamon
½ tsp. ground cloves

Mix thoroughly and store in covered container. Use 1 - 3 tsp. to a cup of boiling water for one cup of tea.

The Shaw family in front of the Ellijay parsonage

Grandmother Is Me

When our first granddaughter, Lyn Turrentine, was born, her mother Joan asked me what Lyn should call me. My reply was "grandmother." And I remember the first time she said "grandmother." I looked around to see what little old lady she was talking to. I wrote:

One day I was a child. I ran
Holding close my mother's hand.
Another day ... so soon away
A little child, I heard her say,
"Grandmother ... see!"
I turned around ... Both left and right.
A little old lady ... was not in sight.
How can it be? ... Grandmother is me!

Where did they go ... The youthful years
With all their joy and all their fears?
They flew away ... On wings of love and tears.
Where did they go ... The youthful years?
They went too fast ... I said with tears.
They flew away ... In beautiful array,
Or so they say ... Like pages turning,
In a treasured book ... And I
... I didn't have time to look.

Where did she go ... that little girl?
The child that once was me?
She slipped away ... To yesterday
While I was looking the other way.
How can it be? ... Grandmother is me!

~RBS~

Look Up

If you could see an inch beyond your nose
I've always heard it said,
You would have planned ... for rainy days
And looked ahead.

You would have known that winter time
Was sure to come
And took no time to laugh and sing
In summer's sun.

And they are right ... they are so right
Enough ... I've always known it's true
That dreaming folks ... and poets
Still get their due.

But when I look beyond myself ... I see
I know ... A place where tiny sparrows sing
And lilies grow.

Arrayed in beauty ... so assured the Father's care,
A place where I can go ... Oh, I've been there.
Oh ... I've been there!

~RBS~

Christmas Gifts

At Christmastime our lists are long
We plan with serious task
To give good gifts to children
Gifts they ask!
"How much more," said Jesus
"Shall God the Father give,
Good Gifts to us, His Children."
Gifts that live!

For persons that "Have everything"
He does not recommend
Like we - "A jeweled bottle top"
Or yet - "A mink trimmed pin."
His gifts cannot be measured
Like those we lay-a-way.
But neither are they smashed or torn
Before New Year's Day.

The gifts of God are packaged
So that we
With eyes for wrappings only
Sometimes never see.
His gifts of joy and gentleness,
Faith, goodness, from above
A personalized gift, engraved
With His incarnate love.

~RBS, 1973~

But the fruits of the Spirit are love, joy, peace, patience, kindness, goodness, faithfulness, gentleness and self-control. ~Galatians 5:22~

If ye then, being evil, know how to give good gifts unto your children, how much more shall your heavenly Father give good gifts to them that ask Him. ~Matthew 7:11~

For God so loved the world, that he gave . . . ~John 3:16~

Christmas at Trinity

At Trinity Church in Rome, Georgia, a live Nativity Scene has become a Christmas tradition. Mary Craven suggested the project in 1957 to make Christmas a more Christian event for children. Her husband Paul, a Trinity member and Rome contractor, built the first set. Today their son, Frank Craven, and his family build the set each year and care for the animals.

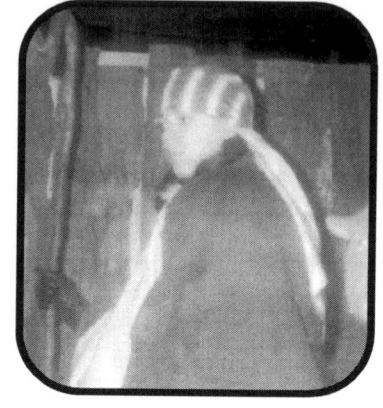

Until we moved to Rome, I had never been very enthusiastic about live Nativity Scenes. But as I watched and participated in the event each Christmas, I began to feel the inspiration that had motivated others to spend long hours in making this annual event "a happening."

It helped to reinforce the real meaning of Christmas just to be a part of the "behind the scenes" planning. This activity included helping to arrange turbans and halos on heads, heating bricks upon which cold wise men and shepherds stood and making hot chocolate or coffee for tired workers.

Debi as a shepherd

Carol as Mary

No one had to ask, "Do you have the Christmas spirit?" It was evident all through the church as everyone joyfully worked together.

Kathy, who had been deaf from birth, was a young teenager when we were there. She dearly loved to play the part of an angel. And she was, in spite of that mischievous twinkle in her eyes and the clever way she had of seeming not to see her parents when they were about to "sign" a reprimand to her.

Christmas at Trinity

Our Nativity scene is alive
In living color too!
With teen-aged Mary dressed
Of course, in blue!

She sits beside the manger
Carol, Beth or Anne,
With Joseph standing by
In brown. He's Bill or Dan.

The shepherds stand alert
With turbans on their heads.
There's Mike and Sam and
Yes, the third is Fred.

The wise men are bedecked
In jeweled crowns that hide -
Or almost hide - the tousled hair
Of Terry, Rob and Clyde.

The angels, Kathy, Fran,
Real girls and truly dear
But they can only qualify
As angels - once a year!

I watch the twisted halos
And am amazed to feel
In spite of pomp and pageantry
They somehow make Him real!

~RBS, 1963~

Happy Birthday Jesus

Birthdays were special occasions in our family when our children were young. The mood was festive and although the gifts were usually insignificant, there was always a gift and a special cake with candles. And singing! The honoree was awakened to the tune of "Happy Birthday to You." One Christmas, four-year-old David asked, "Are we going to sing, 'Happy Birthday Dear Jesus?'"

Beth decorating the Christmas tree in Ellijay

Happy Birthday Dear Jesus

Today with festive fare

We celebrate Your birthday,

With music in the air!

Cakes are baked and waiting

Candles light the tree

Gifts are wrapped and ribboned.

Is there no gift for Thee?

Jesus on Thy birthday morning

I kneel beside Thy creche and see

Love incarnate - God's gift

And bring myself to Thee!

David in Trinity parsonage in Rome

~RBS~

Desserts

Beth, Debi and David celebrating Debi's birthday

Layer Cake from Scratch

The cake the mixes try to imitate

1 cup butter or margarine
2 cups sugar
1 cup milk
3 cups flour
¼ tsp. salt
4 eggs
1½ tsp. baking powder

Cream sugar, salt and butter thoroughly in a large mixing bowl. Add egg yolks, one at a time, into creamed mixture and beat until light and fluffy. Add vanilla.

Sift together flour and baking powder. Add flour and milk alternately to the creamed mixture. Blend well after each addition. Beat egg whites stiff but not dry. Fold into batter. Turn into 2 greased and floured 9 inch cake pans. Bake in 350 degree oven about 35 minutes or until cake tester comes out clean. Turn layers on cooling rack and prepare filling.

Ieula Baird cutting a cake in her kitchen in Porterdale

Ieula Baird's Date Nut Filling

2 cups pecans chopped
1 pkg. dates chopped
2 cups sugar
1 stick margarine
1 large can milk

Cook over medium heat five minutes. Stir constantly. Cool and spread between layers and on top and sides of three cake layers.

Lillian Johnston's Pecan Pie

½ cup sugar
¼ tsp. salt
3 eggs

½ tsp. vanilla
1 cup light corn syrup
1 cup chopped pecans

Beat eggs slightly. Add other ingredients. Mix well. Pour into unbaked pie shell. Bake 45 minutes at 300 degrees.

*Carol, Terry and Debi in
Ellijay parsonage*

Old Fashioned Tea Cakes

1 cup shortening
2 cups sugar
2 eggs
½ cup milk
1 teaspoon vanilla
3 cups self-rising flour

Mix all ingredients together. Add enough flour to make a stiff dough. Roll out until thin. Cut with cookie cutters and put on a cookie sheet. Bake at 400 until brown, about 5-6 minutes.

Junior Evening Fellowship in Ellijay, Georgia. Carol is second from right in the front row. Terrell is 2nd from left in back row.

Ellijay Apple Cake

2 cups sugar
1½ cup salad oil
3 eggs

Combine, beat well and add:

1 tsp. vanilla
3 cups flour - sifted with 1 tsp. baking soda
3 eggs
1 tsp. salt

Then add:
3 cups chopped apples
1 cup nut meats

Pour into 2 greased and floured loaf pans or a sheet cake pan. Bake at 350 degrees for 45 minutes to one hour.

Topping for Ellijay Apple Cake

1 cup light brown sugar
¼ cup evaporated milk
1 stick margarine

Bring to boil and boil 2½ minutes. Pour over hot cake. Each loaf will serve 10 to 12 persons.

Fresh Strawberry Pie

1 baked pie shell

1 pint fresh strawberries (washed and hulled)

Cook together:
1 cup sugar
2 tbsp. corn starch

½ tsp. salt
1 cup boiling water

Boil until thick. Stir in 2 tbsp. strawberry gelatin. Let cool. Slice the berries into baked pie shell. Pour cooled mixture over berries and place in refrigerator. Serve with whipped cream.

Brown Sugar Brownies

2/3 cup melted margarine
1 tsp. vanilla
1 lb. brown sugar
1 cup chopped nuts
3 eggs

2¾ cups flour
2½ tsp. baking powder
½ tsp. salt
1 pkg. chocolate bits or ¾ cup chopped dates.

Mix dry ingredients. Sift over nuts and bits. Add margarine and sugar. Add eggs one at a time. Stir in flour mixture. Pour into greased and floured sheet cake pan. Bake 40 minutes at 350 degrees. Cut into tiny squares while hot.

Lemon Fluff Freeze

3 eggs (separated)
5 tbsp. lemon juice
½ cup sugar
½ pint cream or cold evaporated milk
Graham cracker crumbs

Beat yolks until thick. Add lemon juice. Beat whites stiff. Add sugar. Fold two mixtures together. Whip cream until thick. Fold into mixture. Line pan with crumbs. Add mixture. Sprinkle crumbs on top. Freeze. To serve, cut in squares.

Christmas Candy

¼ cup sweetened condensed milk
½ tsp. salt
1 box confectioners' sugar

1 tsp. vanilla
1 stick margarine
½ cup chopped nuts

Mix together. Roll into marble size balls. Place in refrigerator to harden. Stick a toothpick in each and dip into a mixture of chocolate and equal amount of paraffin melted together in double boiler. Hold in air a minute to dry and they are ready to eat.

Chocolate Pound Cake

3 cups sugar
½ tsp. baking powder
2 sticks margarine
½ tsp. salt
½ cup shortening

1¼ cup milk
6 eggs
2 tsp. vanilla
3 cups flour
½ cup cocoa

Cream shortenings with sugar. Add eggs one at a time and blend well. Sift dry ingredients and add alternately with milk. Add vanilla and bake in a greased and floured tube pan at 325 degrees for 1 hour and 15 min.

Chocolate Frosting

½ cup shortening
2/3 cups milk
2 cups sugar
¼ tsp. salt
¼ cup cocoa
2 tsp. vanilla

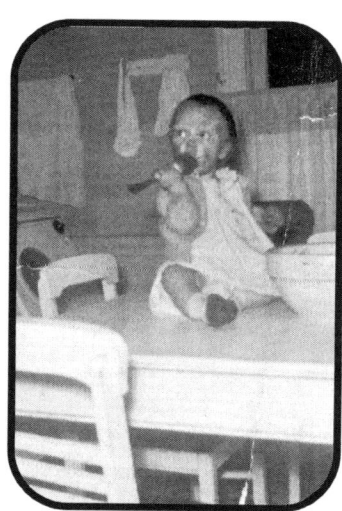

Cook two minutes, stirring constantly. If too thick, add 1 tbsp. cream. Let cool slightly and spread on chocolate pound cake. This is also a good frosting for layer cake.

Beth licking the bowl after Ruth mixed a chocolate cake in the Midway-Sunnyside parsonage kitchen.

Pound Cake

3 cups sugar
½ tsp. baking powder
2 sticks margarine
½ tsp. salt
½ cup shortening

1¼ cup milk
6 eggs
2 tsp. vanilla
3½ cups flour

Cream shortenings with sugar. Add eggs one at a time and blend well. Sift dry ingredients and add alternately with milk. Add vanilla and bake in a greased and floured tube pan at 325 degrees for 1 hour and 15 min.

Kentucky Pound Cake

2½ cups self-rising flour
2½ tsp. cinnamon
1 small can crushed pineapple
1 cup chopped nuts
2 tbsp. water

2 cups sugar
1½ cups corn oil
1½ tsp. nutmeg
4 eggs separated
1 tsp. vanilla

Mix dry ingredients well. Add pineapple, water, oil and egg yolks. Beat whites until stiff and fold in. Pour into greased and floured tube pan. Bake at 325 degrees for 1 hour and 15 minutes.

Blueberry Cobbler

1 stick margarine
1 cup sugar
1 cup self-rising flour
1 cup milk
2 cups sweetened berries or other fruit

Melt butter in shallow baking dish. Mix flour, sugar, and milk. Pour over melted butter. Do not mix. Add fruit. Bake about 45 minutes in 350 degree oven. (*I have used fresh, frozen and canned fruits at various times with good results*).

Aunt Mary
(Mary Baird Shepard)

Aunt Mary's Strawberry Cake

1 box while cake mix (or yellow)
½ cup water
1 small pkg. strawberry gelatin
3 tbsp. flour
½ cup juice from 10 oz. pkg. frozen strawberries
4 eggs
1 cup oil

Mix dry ingredients, adding remaining ingredients.

Bake in two layers.

Icing for Aunt Mary's Strawberry Cake

1 box powered sugar, sifted
4 tbsp. margarine, melted
Strawberries reserved from the 10 oz. pkg.

Mix sugar and berries, adding margarine last. Spread between layers and on top of cake.

Strawberry Trifle

1 round angel food cake
1 large strawberry gelatin
1 large instant vanilla pudding
1 large container Cool Whip
Frozen or fresh strawberries

Beth, Carol, Terry and Debi

Follow package directions for gelatin and pudding. Fold Cool Whip into pudding. Break cake into small pieces. Into a large bowl put gelatin in first. Layer in berries, cake, pudding, about two layers each. Save out a few berries and Cool Whip to garnish. Keep in refrigerator until serving.

Chocolate Chess Pie

1 stick margarine, melted
2 eggs
1¼ cup sugar
Dash of salt
1 tsp. vanilla
1 small can evaporated milt
3 tbsp. cocoa
1 unbaked pie shell

Put first seven ingredients into a blender and blend well. Pour into pie shell and bake for 35-40 minutes at 350 degrees.

Old Fashioned Taffy (Pull Candy)

In my childhood (in the late 1920s and early 1930s), we sometimes got together with our neighbors and made taffy or "pull candy" at our house.

2 cups sugar
½ cup vinegar
½ cup water
2 Tablespoons butter

Bring all ingredients to a boil, cooking until mixture will spin a long thread (or to 275 degrees on a candy thermometer). Remove from heat, add 1 teaspoon vanilla and pour into greased plates until cool enough to handle.

When the candy begins to "set", we would wash and butter our hands, take a little ball of the hot candy (about the size of a small egg), and pull and twist, and sometimes plait it until it began to cool and get hard. Then it would be placed on a buttered plate and cut into sticks of candy.

Lisette's Apple Dumplings

2 pkgs. crescent rolls
2 sticks margarine, melted
1 cup sugar
1 tsp. cinnamon
2 large apples
2 cups ginger ale or Mello Yello

Cut apples into 8 wedges each. Wrap a crescent roll around an apple wedge.
Place in 9 x 13 inch casserole dish. Mix sugar and melted margarine and pour
over rolls. Sprinkle with cinnamon. Pour Mello Yello or ginger ale over all.
Bake at 350 degrees until brown. Let set about 30 minutes before serving

Charles Shaw in his Marine
uniform – World War II

Janice, Joan, Ruth
This photo was taken to send to
Charles when he was serving overseas.

Today

I'd like to have another chance
To live my life once more.
I'd like to take my tests again
I'd make a higher score.
I'd like to have another chance
To use the wisdom gained.
Perhaps I'd then become - in time
The person God ordained.
I can't go back to yesterday,
However poor the score.
But I can have another chance.
Today - I'll try once more.

~RBS, 1975~

I Wish You Love and More!

The following wedding poem was written at the request of my grandson, Steven, and his bride-to-be, La Donna. They asked me to write a poem and read it as part of their beautiful wedding ceremony on June 24, 1990 in the church where her father was pastor. They told me that they had been reading the "Love Chapter of the Bible", 1 Corinthians 13, together.

Though I speak with the tongues of men and of angels, and have not charity, I am become as sounding brass, or a tinkling cymbal. And though I have the gift of prophecy, and understand all mysteries, and all knowledge; and though I have all faith, so that I could remove mountains, and have not love, I am nothing. And though I bestow all my goods to feed the poor, and though I give my body to be burned, and have not love, I am nothing. Love suffereth long, and is kind; love envieth not; love vaunteth not itself, is not puffed up, Doth not behave itself unseemly, seeketh not her own, is not easily provoked, thinketh no evil; Rejoiceth not in iniquity, but rejoiceth in the truth; Beareth all things, believeth all things, hopeth all things, endureth all things. Love never fails.

~1 Corinthians 13:1-7~

A Wedding Poem
"I Wish you Love and More!"

Based on the "Love Chapter of the Bible"

In a world of noisy gongs
And clanging cymbals in the air,
I wish you quiet love and more!
More than human love can bear
That spark of Love Divine
That truly molds two hearts as one
The flame of perfect love.
The essence of God's Son!

In a world of idle, thoughtless words
On tongues of men and poets and seer
I wish you sounds of love and more
More than human love can hear
I wish you covenant with One
Who one day in a baby crèche
The Alpha and Omega spoke
The Word of Love made flesh!

In a world of knowledge unsurpassed
And technology advances
For you I wish a wedding gift more rare
Than instruction kits on love…or classes
The spark of Love Divine,
That truly molds two hearts as one
In perfect faith and hope and love;
The essence of God's Son!

~RBS~

Spring Miracles

One of the Beatitudes Jesus taught is *"Blessed are the meek, for they shall inherit the earth."* This seems to have a broader meaning than merely that mild people, meek as lambs, would ultimately inherit the earth. The French New Testament renders this verse *"Heureusles debonnaires"* – Blessed are the debonair. Debonair is not passive but active, able to take possession, aware.

We lived in the Epworth parsonage near the Druid Hills area of Atlanta from 1970 -1974. The neighborhood was so beautiful in the spring that *National Geographic* featured an aerial view of the area with the dogwoods in bloom.

Meekness is not weakness. Even in times when we have neither the time nor the talent to own a flower garden, we can have ownership of all the sights and fragrances of spring

Charles planted tulips at the parsonage of each church he served.

I took a walk one April day
The earth had turned to Spring
And when I saw the countryside
My heart began to sing!
For I remembered Jesus said:
"Blessed are the meek,
They shall inherit all the earth."
Oh, let me join the meek.
My first draft; daffodils profuse
Flashing gems - they shine
To make the winter landscape
A golden flower mine.
And lavender blankets of "Thrift,"
with wild extravagancy
Have transformed barren slopes into
A Springtime canopy.
Tulips, pansies, hyacinths,
What rare perfume they bring
Glorious resurgence and
Cheerful smells of Spring.
The Dogwood trees were blooming
A blank check from the sod.
I draw up close enough to see
The signature of God.
Oh, I don't need a written deed
To claim my legacy
The flowering earth I hold in trust
All that I see belongs to me!

~RBS~

Autumn Wisdom

The Prophet Isaiah (55:12) talks about mountains and hills breaking forth into singing and trees clapping their hands.

It seems to me the mountains are singing clearer and louder in Autumn than at any other time. It is in the Fall of the year that the mountains call us to see and hear and experience the beauty of the mountains!

John Muir made some interesting comments about trees, not just about trees singing but also preaching! He wrote: "Few are altogether deaf to the preaching of pine trees. Their sermons on the mountains go to our hearts; and if people in general could be got into the woods, even for once, to hear the trees speak for themselves, all difficulties in the way of forest preservation would vanish." ~John Muir, naturalist, explorer, and writer (1838-1914)~

A few years ago, Ken Cook, a meteorologist, spoke to our Retired Pastors group at Simpsonwod United Methodist Center about his flower business in North Georgia. He told us that his dahlias bloom in the Spring and in the Fall. He said that when they bloom again in the Fall, the colors are more vibrant and sparkling than when they bloomed in the Spring.

More vibrant, more sparkling in the Fall? (The photo to the left is only a small vase of the amazingly beautiful autumn blooming dahlias from the garden of Terrell and Sheila Shaw (October 17, 2009)

What about the autumn of life? I wrote a poem. The last verse of my poem is for all of us who are "old" and for the rest of us who are planning on getting a "whole lot older."

Winter is an etching, spring a watercolor, summer an oil painting
and autumn a mosaic of them all.

~Stanley Horowitz~

Autumn Wisdom

I walked into October
And lifted up my ears to hear
The very mountains singing
Choir-robed for praise . . . in Autumn . . . clear . . .

Sunset yellows, burning bush reds.
My heart . . . in awe . . . took off its shoes
And stood on Holy ground to view
Creation's God in Autumn hue . . .

For every tree was clapping
The Doxology . . . lifted high
I think some unseen maestro
Was pointing to the sky!

I heard the mountains singing
With concert voices raised
When every hill pulled out the stops . .
Adorned in breathless Autumn praise ...

I shall long remember this:
The mountains grandest notes are sung
Not in springtime's newness,
But in Autumn's aging tongue.

~RBS~

Winter Silence

On January 12, 1982, a paralyzing snowstorm swept into Georgia. It was reported to be the coldest day of the century. Many motorists were stranded at their places of work. Cars were left on the impassable roads for days. I had gone to the grocery store less than a mile from our parsonage in Forest Park just as the snowflakes started falling. I barely managed to slip and slide back home. For several days, there was nothing to do but stay home.

My whole world is a poem today
Words etched in frozen white
Written out in flakes of snow
And published last night.

I woke to read the beauty
In chiseled litanies.
On library wall with signs displayed,
"No talking - Quiet please."

God stopped me in my tracks today,
Delayed my morning rush.
I whispered at the sight of such
A soundless winter hush.

I tiptoed to a window
That once had framed the sod.
And silently, I read the words,
"Be still and know that I am God."

~RBS, January 14, 1982~

My Song of Praise

Just a year or so before my husband, Charles, had his first heart attack, we were pulling off the expressway to go to our United Methodist parsonage in Austell where we lived at the time.

We saw a man fall down beside the road. We had gotten past him so we had to get to a place to turn around and drive back. Charles asked me to stay in the car until he talked to the man. The man was on crutches with a broken leg in a cast and was falling down drunk.

Charles put him in the car, took him home with us, put him in the shower and helped him get a bath while I washed his clothes and prepared him something to eat. Later Charles was able to get him into a Christian home for alcoholics.

So it is. We come to Jesus just as we are, clothed in the garments of sin, spiritually starving and sick unto death. We are welcomed by Christ (and hopefully by Christians), accepted just as we are, bathed in God's love and forgiveness . . . transformed and clothed in his Grace – indeed given a place at His table of Grace.

I heard Dottie Rambo tell of praying for a brother who had become alcoholic. He was finally won to the Lord and was the inspiration of one of my favorites of all of Dottie's songs:

He Looked Beyond My Fault

Amazing Grace shall always be my song of praise
For it was Grace that bought my liberty.
I do not know just why He came to love me so.
He looked beyond my fault and saw my need.

I shall forever lift mine eyes to Calvary . . .
To view the cross where Jesus died for me.
How marvelous . . . the Grace that caught my falling soul.
He looked beyond my fault and saw my need.

~Dottie Rambo~

Mary and Martha

In 1979, Charles and I visited the Holy Land. One Sunday morning we drove out to the Eastern slope of the Mount of Olives for a worship service. We had a breathtaking view of Jerusalem across the Kidron Valley. Alvis Waite from the South Georgia Conference read the scripture and Charles preached. Afterward we made a pilgrimage to see Lazarus's tomb and the site of the home of Martha, Mary and Lazarus. Who could visit Bethany and not write something about Mary and Martha?

The road to Petra . . .

. . . in Jordan

Mary and Martha

When I was a child
I loved the story best
Of Mary and Martha.
When Jesus was their guest

Martha prepared
The bread and the meat,
While Mary kept sitting
At Jesus feet.

Somehow in the reading,
The thought was inferred
That women, like children,
Should be seen and not heard!

And I thought like a Martha,
Stayed in my place,
Tended my household,
Took care of my face.

Then one day reading further
With a strangely warm heart,
I heard, I really heard, Jesus say
Mary has chosen that good part.

How I long to be Mary
Disciple devout,
But I'm more often Martha
Cumbered about.

Much hurry and serving
I stay on the . . . run,
For a Martha's work
Is never quite done.

But I thank God
For the seasons of special retreat,
When even a Martha
Can sit at His feet!

~*RBS, 1979*~

Mary and Martha

... Martha welcomed Him into her house. And she had a sister called Mary who also sat at Jesus' feet and heard His word. But Martha was distracted with much serving, and she approached Him and said, "Lord, do you not care that my sister has left me to serve alone? Therefore tell her to help me." And Jesus said to her, "Martha, Martha, you are worried and troubled about many things. But one thing is needed, and Mary has chosen that good part, which will not be taken away."

~Luke 10:38-42~

A Ballad for My Mother

My mother grew old. . .
had lines etched in her face
Worked hard all her life. .
with uncommon grace
She lived by the Bible. . .
And I'd visit awhile
She taught me her secret. . .
of life with a smile

CHORUS:

Ieula Ann Dick Baird

She said. . . Today is the first day
Of the rest of your life.
Don't borrow trouble
With yesterday's strife.
Take time. . . smell the flowers
That's worth living for
Then pick up each new day
And fill it with joy!

2. Widowed while young. . .
Mama worked in the mill
Washed on a scrub-board. . .
Brought wood up a hill
She sang as she labored. . .
to stay out of debt
And taught me this lesson. . .
I'll never forget

3. One day I said, Mama . . .
Your life has been hard
You've buried two babies. . .
Out in the church yard

You've known all the heartache
of struggling for bread,
She smiled through her tears
and these words she said:

CHORUS:
Today is the first day
Of the rest of your life.
Don't borrow trouble
With yesterday's strife.
Take time. . . smell the flowers
That's worth living for
Then pick up each new day
And fill it with joy!

4. Her old fashioned tea cakes. . .
We ate the last crumb
Her old fashioned flowers. . .
She had a green thumb.
She lived by the Bible. . .
each day and each mile
She taught me her secret. . .
of life with a smile!

~RBS, 1982~

Non-Food
Recipes

In the Ellijay parsonage: l-r Terry, Charles holding David, Ruth, Carol, Debi, Beth

A Good Furniture Cleaner

Boiled linseed oil
Household vinegar
Turpentine

Use equal amounts of each ingredient and mix together to clean antique or other furniture.

Finish Remover

Boiled Linseed Oil
Turpentine
Denatured Alcohol

Use equal amounts of each to remove old finish from wood. *(These recipes were given to me by an antique dealer).*

Play Dough

1 cup salt
½ cup corn starch
½ cup boiling water

Mix well and cook over low heat, stirring constantly until dough is too stiff to stir. Let cool and knead until pliable. Add cake coloring to make desired color as you knead dough.

Christmas dinner at Mama and Daddy Shaw's house in Milstead, Georgia (Grady and Lillian Shaw)

Where to look in the Bible

If you...

Are facing a crisis

Job 28:12-28, Proverbs 8; Isaiah 55

Are bereaved

I Corinthians 15; I Thessalonians 4:15 - 5:28; Revelation 21-22

Are bored

II Kings 5; Job 38; Psalm 103; Ephesians 3

Are challenged by opposing forces

Ephesians 6; Philippians 4

Are jealous

Psalms 49; James 3

Bear a grudge

Luke 6; II Corinthians 4; Ephesians 4

Have experienced severe losses

Colossians 1; I Peter 1

Need forgiveness

Matthew 21; Luke 15

Homilies and Meditations

Poetry Words

When I was in high school, we were required to prepare a deck of vocabulary cards. We wrote a word on the front of the 3-by-5 card and the definition of the word on the back. We carried these cards with us to study new words and make them a part of our vocabulary.

As adults, our stacks of vocabulary cards grow taller and taller. My stack of words kept growing as I moved into college and later into seminary. Those of us who enrolled in Candler School of Theology (Emory University) remember our first class when Dr. William Mallard said, "When you go home today and you are asked what you learned in seminary you can say, 'Uh… Hermeneutics.'" Some students found ways to keep saying "hermeneutics." Mallard defined the word as "the science of the interpretation of Scripture or method of exegesis."

I want us to imagine that each word in our vocabulary is on a 3-by-5 card and the cards are all stacked in rows on a table. As we speak, words are selected. Words are used to communicate, to convince, to tell a story and to relay a message. All the words in our English language use only 26 letters. Everything we need to know, all the words used to express all meaning, can be said or written using only 26 letters. Yet it takes a thick dictionary to hold them all.

And we are sometimes speechless – inadequate when it comes to selecting the right word or combination of words and putting the words together to really communicate with one another. I suppose everyone who has an interest in communication struggles with finding the right word – the correct combination of words. We struggle with putting meaning into words. If we are a writer or a minister or teacher we could say, "Words are the tools of our trade." Churchill said, "Words are really the only thing that lasts forever." He continued to tell us, "Short words are best and old words are best of all." Words are powerful! John Kennedy said of Churchill, "He mobilized the English language and sent it into battle."

Recently I had occasion to go to Fort McPherson. I stopped at the gate to get a pass. Two young soldiers, a man and a woman, were in the gate house. They were talking loudly in sounds that sounded like serious argument. The young man came over to see my driver's license. As he was filling out my pass, I decided to ask about it. I asked if they were fighting or just clowning around. He said, "Oh we were just talking." Just talking? It got me to thinking about language ... words ... rhetoric.

Which comes first, language or thoughts? Do words form our belief systems or do concepts? Do concepts (from the depths of our subconscious) give birth to our language – our rhetoric?

Words! In these few minutes – as I have been speaking, I have taken a stack – a pile of words – short words – old words – words that lend variety – and arranged them as prose. Prose is words which tend toward variety. Walter Ong made an interesting statement. He said, "Hearing is a better metaphor for the relationship between God and human ... than seeing. Hearing," he said, "is being surrounded by God's Word."

Poetry or verse in our culture is words arranged with repetition in their accent rhythm and which tend toward uniformity rather than variety. The value of poetry is not confined to what is said. Equally as important is the language used – the words! Not just the meaning but being "surrounded by the words."

To say that Ruth in the Old Testament was homesick is not the same as saying with Keats, "She stood in tears amid the alien corn." Emily Dickinson could have said: "Life is short." But we catch our breath to hear: "I had no time to hate because the grave would hinder me ... and life is not so ample ... I could finish enmity."

I close this meditation with some words, some theology vocabulary words ... arranged as verse, poetry. And I suppose it goes back to our society being inundated with words...and the first verse in the book of John. John tells us the prophets of old came, generation after generation, with words about God. But many could not hear. Then one day in the city of Bethlehem the Word was made flesh and came among us. And we beheld his glory.

While I was a student in seminary, I wrote a poem about some of our theology words to read in a class assignment. The professor asked to publish it in the *Candler Chronicle*, a monthly paper for students. I titled it "Tower of Babel."

Tower of Babel

I pile my poetry words
Up high
And stand and gaze
Up to the sky.

And higher
High as eye can see
Hermeneutics, Exegesis,
Theodicy!

Early on Diversity
The "cutting edge."
Plurality.
Then add "Process Theology"
Post-Structuralist
Eschatology.

I clap my hands
My words have power,
I dance around,
My poetry tower.

Confusion
Babel tumbles down.
My words lie silent
On the ground.
And kneeling there
in wordless loss,
I find the "WORD"
Beneath a cross!

~RBS~

Ash Wednesday

When our daughter, Deborah, was critically ill at age 2 months, her Daddy and I sat in the waiting room of the hospital where other people with sick children were waiting.

If you have spent many days in a hospital waiting room, you realize how you begin to interact with people. You listen to their stories and tell yours. You become concerned about their loved ones and appreciate their concern for yours. Each individual patient is precious to someone.

Charles and I were so distraught that someone asked, "Is she your only child?" I replied, "She is our fifth child, but she is our only Debi."

Jesus came to earth to tell us the amazing news that each individual one of us is precious to God. We each have our own fingerprint, our own voice accent, our own DNA. God so loved each one of us that he sent Jesus that whosoever believes in Him will not perish but have everlasting life. (John 3:15)

The Pharisees thought God rejoiced in the death of "sinners." In Luke 15, Jesus tells us there is joy in heaven when each one of us repents of our wandering and believes this greatest Good News the world has ever heard! (Luke 15:10)

Ash Wednesday begins Lent and the believer's journey to Holy Week and Easter. It is a journey of individual repentance and prayer. In the Service of Ashes, we kneel at the altar and the pastor marks the sign of the cross in ashes on our forehead. The ashes are to remind us that our physical body is dying. The sign of the cross is to remind us that we are more than our physical body.

What we call" death" does not have the last word over what God calls "life." It is Ash Wednesday but Easter is coming!

Prayer: *Father, during this Lenten season, help each one of us to kneel at the cross in humility and to arise in the strength of knowing who we are in Christ Jesus our Lord. Amen.*

Do you know about Easter?

Mark 16:1-7

Now when the Sabbath was past, Mary Magdalene, Mary the mother of James, and Salome brought spices, that they might come and anoint Him. Very early in the morning, on the first day of the week, they came to the tomb when the sun had risen. And they said to themselves, "Who will roll away the stone from the door of the tomb for us?" But when they looked up, they saw that the stone had been rolled away for it was very large. And entering the tomb, they saw a young man clothed in a long white robe sitting on the right side, and they were alarmed. But he said to them, "Do not be alarmed. You seek Jesus of Nazareth, who was crucified. He is risen! He is not here. See the place where they laid Him. But go, tell His disciples and Peter that He is going before you into Galilee; there you will see Him, just as He said to you."

~Mark 16:1-7~

Do You Know About Easter?

But go, tell the disciples and Peter that Jesus is going ahead of you
to Galilee: there you will see Him, just as He said to you.
~ Mark 16:7~

One of the stories making the email rounds is about an elderly woman named Edith. The story has Edith asking individuals at every opportunity, "Do you know about Easter?" The opening scene in the story has Edith in her doctor's waiting room, asking a young woman, "Do you know about Easter?" and then telling the woman about Jesus and leading her to Christian faith. Meanwhile, Edith's doctor is preparing to tell her that tests prove a malignancy in her body. Her time is short. Edith's final scenes are in the hospital. She is dying but still looking for every opportunity to happily ask everyone who comes in her room, "Do you know about Easter?"

Edith is kind and cheerful but the cynical head nurse, Eleanor, is impatient and verbal with what she calls "Edith's fanaticism." Edith's major prayer is that she will not die until she gets the "go ahead" to talk to Eleanor about Easter and to lead her to faith in Christ. This complete turn-around for Eleanor does finally happen as the nurse observes Edith's joy in Christ and her consistent life and testimony.

The last scene in this drama has nurse Eleanor walking out of the hospital room after Edith's death and asking the first person she meets in the hallway, "Do you know about Easter?"

Easter is not just one Sunday but a season of seven Sundays on the church calendar. Indeed, every Sunday is Easter. The reason for meeting on Sunday instead of the Jewish Sabbath is to celebrate that first Easter.

Mark tells us[1] that very early in the morning on the first day of the week, some of the women came to the tomb to anoint the body of Jesus against the decay. To their fear and dismay, they found an empty tomb. This was the last straw in a series of tragedies. Jesus had been beaten, crucified, dead and buried. Now the body had been stolen away. What else could go wrong? Jesus had told his disciples that he was to die and in three days rise again. But they had their own agenda for throwing off the yoke of Rome and winning freedom for their generation. They could not believe Jesus came to bring salvation to the whole world - Gentiles as well as the Jews. They could not believe Jesus came to bring salvation, not only for their generation but also for every generation. The disciples were too busy arguing over nonessentials like "Who would sit on the right hand and on the left when Jesus finally got the Romans off their backs and established His own kingdom?"

When my husband Charles and his Marine buddies came home from the South Pacific at the end of World War II, he said he would never forget the sight of the Golden Gate Bridge in San Francisco. He came up on deck very early to get a glimpse of the bridge as soon as it came in view. War veterans who spent time in the South Pacific still see the Golden Gate Bridge as one of the most beautiful sights in the world. They see it as the gateway to home and the gateway to the free world.

I read a story recently about a veteran who had stopped overnight in San Francisco just to see the historic bridge. He went out early in the morning, but to his dismay the bridge was enveloped in fog. Then just before he had to leave, the fog began to lift, and he could see the upright piers and all that lay between but nothing of the anchorage at either end. He could see the suspension span but not the massive supports that held it up. Life is like that. It comes out of an eternity we cannot see and leads into an eternity we do not know. We just see from birth to death, and it is so very short. Like the early disciples, we worry.

When is a Person Not a Person?

When I was a student at Georgia State University, a student in one of my classes told us about her mother who had Alzheimer's disease. She said, "I looked at her and I thought, 'That's not my mother.'"

We have all had experiences when a person did not seem to be themselves. I began to think about this question of when a person is not the person they have been. This mother was in the same physical body that had given birth to her daughter, had the same hands that had fed her and looked after her needs, and had the same feet that had run to protect her child from danger. Why was she not now her mother? What this girl was really saying is that there is more to life than the physical. There is another dimension to life.

Christopher Reeve was asked what he had learned from being paralyzed. He said he had learned that "we are not our bodies." Christopher may or may not have known it, but this is what Easter is all about. There is more to life than the physical aspect.

Another Reality

We must be prepared to see this other dimension. In other words, Jesus promised his followers that what we call death will not have the final word over what God calls life. The Easter message is that there is more to life than "eat, sleep and work so you can retire early with a good pension."

Job's ancient question, "If a man die shall he live again?" was finally answered from an open grave by Jesus Christ when He walked out of that grave saying, "Because I live, you shall live also."

As a mother, I like the analogy of birth that I first heard Dr. Paul Echols use when he was pastor of First Presbyterian in Atlanta in the 1970s.[2] It put into words some of the thoughts I had had, and it speaks to my logical mind because I believe we accept the Gospel of Jesus Christ by faith, but it is not a blind faith. There are reasons to believe. I believe with Elton Trueblood that there are three areas that need to be cultivated if faith is to be a living faith: the inner life of devotion, the intellectual life of rational thought, and the outer life of human service.[3]

I believe that God is calling some of us to address this area of rational thought as well as the other two. We know our life began in the watery warm world of our mother's womb. In Biology we learned that in the beginning we looked like a speck of transparent jelly. But the body, the mind, the spirit, the emotions ... all the vast potentialities of life were hidden away in that tiny dot of transparent computer-like genetic information ... tiny as a grain of sand.

As an unborn baby, we adapted to the environment of the womb. Had we been aware of it, we would have been frightened at the possibilities of leaving this secure environment of the womb for an outside world. In the womb we lived without breathing. How could we possibly live by breathing? In the womb we lived without light. How could we possibly live with all that light shinning around us? In the womb we lived in water. How could we possibly survive with air all around us instead of water? Frightening possibility! We'd be like a fish out of water...dead! It makes sense. Being born out of the womb would certainly seem like death. (We come onto the world crying while everyone else is smiling when they hear that first cry.)

How in the world could an unborn child know that it is necessary to leave the womb to be born into a larger world? How could we have known that the womb is just a preparation place for a larger world? In the darkness of our mother's womb, eyes were being formed for light we had never seen. In the stillness, ears were being formed ... fashioned for sounds we had never heard. In that airless environment, lungs were being formed for oxygen we had never breathed. In our mother's womb our brain cells were being prepared for thoughts we had never had. And finally we were born. And here we are ... in this big world on the other side of birth.

What if our world is a big womb: This world of spring flowers and sunshine, of tornados and floods, this world of loving care ... and wars ... and crime ... and pain ... and death ... and people who say, "How can a God of love allow pain and untimely deaths?" What if we are being fashioned and prepared for another world, a world as different from this one as this one is different from our mother's womb?

Something More

There is something about the very structure of this world that whispers to me and to you, "There's something more." There is more to life than just what we are able to see and touch and handle. As a child we first sensed this when we learned to count. We quickly learned there is no stopping place. There is always one more number. Infinity! The same is true of every human discipline ... History ... Electronics ... Micro-Biology ... Botany. There is something uncanny about infinity. Science keeps documenting our intuitions about infinity.

For example look at the human ear that was formed in the womb for things it could not hear there. The ear is an amazing receiver set, picking up sounds between sixteen cycles and eighteen thousand cycles a second ... a range of eleven octaves. Radios and dogs and bats keep reminding us that what we hear is only a little of all the sounds around us. Our eyes were formed in our mother's womb for things we could not see in the womb. With normal eyesight, we see all the glorious rainbow colors of nature but no more. But we know that there is more than our eyes can see. There is infra-red at one end of the scale and ultra-violet at the other end. Beyond that there are X-rays ... gamma rays ... cosmic rays ... and the Lord only knows what else. And that is the point. The Lord alone knows what else.

We are learning a little. But the Lord alone knows it all. But we do have the equipment built into us right now to know that we hear and see only a small amount of the world's sights and sounds. Equipment like ... untiring curiosity ... our sensitive spirits ... our believing hearts that hold firmly to things we cannot quite understand. So when Paul tells us, "Eye has not seen, ear has not heard, neither has it entered into the heart of man the things that God has prepared for those who love him," with Paul, I believe!

Decide to Believe

This is the first step ... the decision to believe. And I feel a great sadness for fragile, dying human beings who ball up their puny little fists and say "no" to God's truth. I feel sad for people who say, "This world is all I know ... I'm not going to believe in a world I cannot see with my physical eyes."

On that first Easter, the disciples had grieved for three days. God had stood aside and let them kill the physical body of the only sinless person who ever lived. But just as he said, on the third day Jesus was raised, Jesus was alive! They saw him. They ate with him. They knew him.

He was alive in a body they recognized ... but a body without limitations ... a body that could walk through doors and be ascended into heaven.

Do you know about Easter? What God did once in a graveyard in Jerusalem, he can and will do on a grand scale for all of us who know Jesus as Savior and Lord. Paul reminds us, "Jesus is the first fruits of the resurrection." The first fruits! Against all odds the terminal shall be made alive. God came down and wept with us on Good Friday ... so that some glad morning we will laugh with Him. Alleluia Christ is alive. He is risen indeed!

Notes
[1] Mark 16:1-7

[2] The analogy of the baby in the womb is from a sermon by Dr. Paul Echols, pastor of First Presbyterian Church in Atlanta, 1977- 1988. I do not remember if he gave a footnote to the analogy.

[3] Elton Trueblood. *A Place to Stand.* p.18

Love in Every Language

Acts 2:1-13

When the day of Pentecost had fully come, they were all with one accord in one place. And suddenly there was a sound from heaven, as of a rushing mighty wind, and it filled the whole house where they were sitting. Then there appeared to them divided tongues, as of fire, and one sat on each one of them. And they were all filled with the Holy Spirit and began to speak in other tongues, as the Spirit gave them utterance. And there were dwelling in Jerusalem Jews, devout men, from every nation under heaven, and when the sound occurred, the multitudes came together, and were confused, because everyone heard them speak in his own language. Then they were all amazed and marveled, saying to one another, "Look, are not all these who speak Galileans? And how is it that we hear, each in our own language in which we were born? Parthians, Medes and Elamites, those dwelling in Mesopotamia, Judea and Cappadocia, Pontus and Asia. Phrygia and Oamphylia, Egypt and parts of Libya adjoining Cyrene, visitors from Rome, both Jews and Proselytes. Cretans and Arabs, we hear them speaking in our own tongues the wonderful works of God." So they were all amazed and perplexed, saying to one another, "Whatever could this mean?" Others mocking said, "They are full of new wine."

~Acts 2:1-13~

Love in Every Language

Acts 2:1-13

Pentecost

And at this sound the crowd gathered and were amazed, because each one heard them speaking in the native language of each.
~Acts 2:6~

Pentecost is about "Love in every language, straight from the heart of God." Pentecost concludes the seven Sundays of Easter, because the resurrection of Jesus has its promise fulfilled in the giving of the Holy Spirit.

Shortly before Jesus ascended into heaven, he instructed his disciples to wait in Jerusalem for the Holy Spirit. The book of Acts gives us a cameo picture of the life changing experience and vitality of the 120 men and women disciples as they gathered to observe the feast of Pentecost and to prayerfully wait in Jerusalem for the coming of the Holy Spirit – just as Jesus had instructed them to do.

When we read Acts 2, we know it sounds a little different from our way of having church. In fact, there was so much excitement that people looking on accused them of being drunk.[1] I do not think anyone would come in our church today and accuse us of being drunk. They might more likely accuse us of being dead.

We have all heard the story about the man who dropped dead in church one Sunday. They called 911 and the paramedics rushed in and hauled out twelve people before they got the dead one.

I was baptized as an infant and grew up in the Methodist Church. But I do not remember being taught much about the Holy Spirit.

Of course, I might have been like the little girl Dr. Tom Long tells about. When Dr. Long was teaching a Confirmation Class and he came to

Pentecost he proceeded to tell the children that "Pentecost was when the church was in a group and the Holy Spirit landed on them like tongues of fire on their heads."

The children took all this in stride, all but one little girl who looked wide-eyed and said: "Gosh, Rev. Long, I must have been absent that Sunday."

In the church I grew up in we had Sunday night services but we were back home after about an hour. The Pentecostal Church on the edge of town was still going strong at 8:30, 9:30, 10:30 … and all over town we could hear their singing and shouting and everyone praying at the same time.

Some people laughed at these people because this was a little uncomfortable. My mother did not allow me to laugh but she said it was "extremism" and "fanaticism."

But one thing I respected about these people is they were willing to be "different." We in the mainline churches try so hard to fit in with anything Hollywood and the popular media send down the pike, and sometimes we just reflect the views of the society around us rather than setting Christ-like standards.

We adult Christians are letting our children down when we do not give them information and instructions to offset the life damaging sexual messages and self-serving alcohol propaganda they are getting daily in the media and even in some of our schools.

A Miracle of Language

But my mother was right, at least somewhat right, in her assessment of that particular branch of Pentecostalism in our town. In our text, it was not an unknown tongue, as these people taught, but a miracle of language.

The work of the Holy Spirit in this Bible lesson as well as in the Gospels is to bring about right relationships! The Holy Spirit does not create chaos or confusion. It creates love and community to bring the good news of God's love and salvation to people everywhere. The fire of the Holy Spirit is the source empowering us for ministry and for making disciples, as it was for these 120 disciples in our text.

Visiting in Jerusalem for this feast of Pentecost were Jewish people from all over the world. When these visitors heard the commotion coming from where the Christians had gathered, they were curious and went over to see what was going on.

And they heard the Christians speaking in foreign languages about the great things God had done in Jesus Christ ... and miracle of miracle, they understood in their own language. Miracle of miracles, thousands were added to the church that day.

What the Holy Spirit began that day was an extension of his work among God's people in fulfilling the promise of Jesus in John 14, 15, and 16.

John tells us in chapter 14: Jesus and the twelve are gathered in the upper room. The earthly Jesus is beginning his "goodbye" to his twelve disciples. Jesus begins with the verse we often hear at funerals, "Let not your hearts be troubled." In our language...the Holy Spirit ... the Paracletus ... translates to us, not as just one word ... but many ... "comforter, counselor, helper, encourager, the spirit of truth, someone to stand alongside."

A World of Fear

Since 9/11 we are living in a world of fear. Oh, how we need a "comforter." How we need a "counselor." How we need this "spirit of truth." I heard the story of a little girl in the days when people rode trains with sleepers. The child was put to bed in a top bunk and was very fearful in her strange surroundings, so her daddy told her that God would watch over her.

As everyone got quiet trying to sleep, the fearful child called out, "Mommy, are you there?" The mother assured her she was there. A little later, she called out louder, "Daddy, are you there?" The father tried to reassure her that he was nearby also. After this went on for a while one of the other passengers in the sleeper car lost his patience and said, "Yes, we are all here. Your mommy's here. Your daddy's here, your brother, and all your aunts and cousins. Now please settle down and go to sleep."

The little girl was silent for a moment and then quietly asked, "Mommy, was that God?"

Jesus, in offering us His Holy Spirit, does not treat us like frightened children, not impatiently saying "Shut up and get quiet, I'm giving you whatever you want." Sometimes God has to say "no" to our requests ... like a loving parent who understands our needs and who wants to "grow us up." Part of the work of the Holy Spirit is to grow us up to "Christian maturity"... maturity that manifests itself with love in every language.

I am a longtime student and taught Methodist and Christian history in many of the churches where my husband was pastor. The early Methodist circuit riders rode west with the first settlers in this country and their spirit-filled sermons were used to change the face of America. There is at least one Methodist Church in every county in the United States.

I am told most early Methodist sermons had four points. First, all of us are sinners. None of us are predestined to be lost. Second, all of us can be saved. Third, all of us can know we are saved ("the doctrine of assurance"). The fourth point had to do with the work of the Holy Spirit in daily life. That is, that people can live like "Christian" people. This is not "sinless perfection" but "perfect love" or "Christian maturity."

John Wesley talked about having his heart "strangely warmed" and referred to the Holy Spirit later as "perfect love" — not always perfect judgment or perfect ability — but perfect intentions and "perfect love" for God and others.

I like the story of the little boy who was tagging along in a field as his dad was plowing on a hot humid day. Soon the little boy ran to the house to get his dad a glass of ice water. He returned to the field smiling as he gave the glass to his dad. The dad noticed the little boy's muddy fingers had been holding on the inside of the glass and mud was seeping down inside the large glass of water. The child's intentions were perfect. His love for his dad was perfect. But his performance, his ability, sometimes like ours, was not perfect. The boy's father took the glass and thankfully drank every drop of the water.

In the United Nations, I am told, modern technology has now been perfected to the degree that each representative has ear phones rigged in such a way that a person can be speaking in French and the English and American representatives hear it in English. The Spanish people hear it in their native language, and so do those who speak German. All the delegates hear in their native language.

When I read about this technology I thought, "Praise God, the Lord knew how to speak His love in every language 2,000 years before the computer people in the United Nations perfected that kind of technology."

When we understand the complicated mechanism of articulation through the system of the brain, and how difficult it is for us to understand one another - even when we speak the same language - we begin to understand what a marvelous thing happened on the day of Pentecost.

These fearful Christians were so filled and under the influence of God's Holy Spirit that God was able to utilize their mechanism of speech ... to enable the believer to articulate God's love in languages they had not learned previously.

God Opened a Door and Pushed Me

Both Charles and I recognized my call to preach early on ... in 1975. He, as pastor, and the church (Park Street UMC) recommended me for license to preach, which was then and still is the starting point for ordained ministers in our United Methodist Church.

Charles began to have health problems and after a second heart attack and bypass surgery he retired on disability in 1983. A year later the District Superintendent, Rev. Harold Gray, needed someone to fill in at Rico Church in Palmetto and called one Sunday morning and asked Charles to go down that morning to preach and conduct the service. He did and kept preaching every Sunday except on two occasions when he asked me to go down and preach.

Charles preached his last sermon the first Sunday in advent in 1986 and three days later went home to be with the Lord. Two weeks later the D.S. called me and told me the congregation had asked to have me appointed to finish the conference year. The Bishop and Cabinet agreed. Would I do it? After much prayer, I knew I would be in ministry somehow. I knew this was a door the Lord wanted me to walk through.

In spite of much grief and other responsibility, I began as their pastor the 4th Sunday in Advent and continued while I started and finished the three-year course for a Master of Divinity degree at Candler School of Theology at Emory.

During my over 20 years now as a preacher, I have sought to learn how to communicate this good news of Jesus. The love and power of God in the hearts of people are able to bring people together across all kinds of barriers.

There was a best seller a few years ago entitled, *Men are from Mars, Women are from Venus*.[2] None of us who are married or have ever been married will disagree. Men and women are fascinated with one another but we certainly do not always understand one another. However, on the day of Pentecost and since, the Holy Spirit enabled men and women to better understand one another and to love one another in spite of differences.

The Holy Spirit enables people, one by one, who look different from one another and who speak different languages to love one another. It is not our ability, but our availability to the Holy Spirit of God that the Lord uses to reach people. Amen.

Notes
[1] Acts 2:1-13 Pentecost Sunday.

[2] John Gray. *Men are from Mars, Women are from Venus*.

How Jacob
Became Israel

Genesis 32:22-31

Jacob wrestling with the angel

And Jacob arose that night and took his two wives, his two female servants, and his eleven sons, and crossed over the ford at Jabbok. He took them, sent them over the brook, and sent over what he had. Then Jacob was left alone and a Man wrestled with him until the breaking of day. Now when He saw that He did not prevail against Jacob, He touched the socket of his hip, and the socket of Jacob's hip was out of joint as He wrestled with him. And He said, "Let me go, for the day breaks," but Jacob said, "I will not let You go unless You bless me." So He said to him, "What is your name." He said, "Jacob." And he said, "Your name shall no longer be called Jacob, but Israel, for you have struggled with God and with men and have prevailed." Then Jacob asked saying, "Tell me Your name, I pray." And He said, "Why is it that you ask about My Name?" And He blessed him there. So Jacob called the name of the place Peniel; "for I have seen God face to face, and my life is preserved." Just as he crossed over Peniel, the sun rose on him, and he limped on his hip.

~Genesis 32: 22-31~

How Jacob Became Israel

Genesis 32: 22-31

*And he said, "Your name shall no longer be called Jacob, but Israel, for you have
struggled with God and with men and have prevailed."*
~ Genesis 32:28~

A few years ago, I was visiting with an older couple. They had two
grown children - a son and a daughter - and grandchildren. In the course
of the conversation the man, a Mr. Edwards, told me, "I've finally
conquered my 'want-er." I was not sure what he meant by "want-er."

He explained that he had grown up during the great depression.
All his life he had worked hard. He had struggled for money and the
things money could buy. He had managed to buy a nice house, fine
furnishings, a new car and truck. He and his wife lived on several acres of
land. He said no matter how much he accumulated there was always
something else he needed or wanted. But now, he told me, even though
he did not have all the things he had previously wanted, he no longer
wanted anything else. He had conquered his want-er!

I thought of Mr. Edwards as I studied the life of Jacob. Jacob was
a want-er. We are introduced to Jacob in Genesis 25:26, the day he was
born as the second born of twins. The Bible tells us Jacob came forth out
of Rebekah's womb grabbing hold of his twin brother's heel.

In those days, you remember, the laws of primogeniture brought a
great deal of advantage to the first-born son. So we get a picture of the
pre-born Jacob grabbing hold of his twin brother's heel as if he was trying
to pull Esau back in, so he could get out first.[1]

Being a mother, grandmother and now a great-grandmother, I am
a soft touch when it comes to babies. I can honestly say, "I have never
seen a baby I did not like." If I am in a mall and see a baby, I always turn
my head and smile. To me, babies are more beautiful than even lovely
landscapes.

But even as a newborn baby, Jacob does not appear likeable. This first picture of Jacob as a grabber, always wanting and grabbing to be first in everything is not a pretty picture.

Jacob Wants It All

So we see Jacob as a grasper from birth and we do not get out of chapter 25 where we first meet him until we find him taking advantage of the weak and hungry and apparently thoughtless Esau by buying his brother's birthright for a bowl of lentil soup.[2]

You've heard the story of Esau coming in from the field, tired and hungry. Jacob had prepared some lentil soup and Esau asked his brother for some of the soup. Jacob told Esau he would sell the soup in return for the birthright.

Esau reasoned that he was about to die of hunger so the birthright would not help him anyway, so for "immediate gratification" he exchanged his birthright for a bowl of soup. But the plot thickens and the story becomes more sordid. In those days, not only the birthright but a Father's blessing was of immense value - supernatural value. For the wily Jacob – well, kids today would call him a "jerk" – it was not enough that he had the birthright; he just had to have the "blessing" also. Jacob wanted it all! So with the help of Rebekah, his mother, he deceived his blind father, Isaac, and stole his brother's blessing.

The importance placed on a father's blessing is recorded down through the annals of history in the desperate cry of Esau, "Hast thou but one blessing, my father? Bless me, even me also, oh my father."

There was no blessing left for Esau. Jacob wanted it all. Jacob had taken it all! Esau threatened to kill Jacob. So in fear for his life, Rebekah packed Jacob off to his Uncle Laban. [3]

Jacob almost met his match for trickery in Uncle Laban, who became his father-in-law. Jacob fell in love with the beautiful Rachael. Laban made Jacob work seven years for Rachael which, the Bible tells us, Jacob gladly did because of his great love. But Laban tricked Jacob and in the marriage customs of that time and place, he substituted his older daughter Leah in the marriage bed. So we find Jacob working another seven years for Rachael.

Most of us have heard about the Old Testament patriarchs, Abraham, Isaac and Jacob. We probably remember more about Abraham … how he went from his home in Ur of the Chaldees in answer to the call of God.

We are told how God promised Abraham that his and Sarah's descendents would be as numerous as all the stars he could see on a clear night and how his descendents would be a blessing to the whole world.

Even though Sarah was well past menopause and Abraham was ten years older, we read that Abraham believed God and it was accounted to him as righteousness. Abraham kept believing the promise of God even as the years kept passing before their son Isaac was finally born. (Genesis 19).

The Covenant in the Hands of Jacob

When we get down to Chapter 32, Abraham and Isaac are off the scene and the covenant is in the hands of grandson Jacob. And Jacob — like some second and third generation Christians today — was not concerned about a relationship with God. Jacob has his own agenda. Jacob, the grandson of Abraham, was reaping the benefits of the covenant. But, as we have already talked about, he wanted to live life his way.

When we pick up the scripture lesson in Genesis 32, some twenty years have passed after Jacob's flight away from the angry threats of Esau. Personally, if I had been writing the story of Jacob, when he finally changed and became a part of the covenant, I might have left out or soft-pedaled some of the story. But the Bible tells it all … warts and all.

The story of Jacob is a story of winning and losing, of failure and success. It is a story of family intrigue. It is a mystery story. It is a story of a broken relationship with a brother and consequently a broken relationship with God.[4] It is the story of how Jacob became Israel.

The Story of How Jacob Became Israel

Jacob was coming home from years of absence. He had prospered greatly and reappeared as a person of success with his two wives, Leah and Rachael, two handmaidens and eleven sons. In Jacob's preparation for the reunion with Esau, we see the same old calculating Jacob. He divided his camp and sent presents on ahead to hopefully appease his improvident brother who had so easily been talked out of his birthright.

As I read the story of Jacob's all night struggle, as a student of Methodist history, I thought about the old time Methodist altar call, where people were told to "pray through." Reading Jacob's story from several translations, he seemed to have "prayed through" that dark night at the river Jabbok.

Jacob's prayer of desperation came when he started home to face the music, and he realized he had run out of slick tunes. While Jacob was on his way back home, he appealed to the God he met at Bethel on the way out … the God who summoned him home. Jacob finally confessed to God that he was not worthy of the blessing he stole from his brother.

It was time to face the brother he has wronged. "Wronged" is too mild a word here for the reprehensible - we would say "criminal" - act of deceiving a dying father and stealing from a weaker brother. It makes the prodigal son look like a saint.

So the next picture we see is not one of God running out to embrace him as he did the prodigal son that Jesus tells us about in Luke 15. Instead we see an "all night struggle" in the darkness of the brook Jabbok.

The Scripture does not tell us the identity of the mysterious stranger who wrestles all night with Jacob; but after it is over, Jacob testified that he had seen God face to face.

The God Jacob wrestled with at the brook Jabbok shows a different side of God ...not the promise-filled aspect of the God he met at Bethel, when he saw the ladder reaching down from heaven and heard God's promise to him because of his grandfather, Abraham.

As C.S. Lewis reminds us; "God whispers to us in our pleasures and shouts to us in our sorrows." God whispered his promises to Jacob at Bethel. However, when we get down to the struggles that changed Jacob ... changed him as a person ... receiving a new name and a new nation, God shouted to Jacob.

We often define ourselves by what we do. Jacob was defined and had defined himself as a trickster but he was tired of being schizophrenic. The mysterious struggle was a two way struggle. We are not told much about the wrestling ... only that it lasted all night.

At the breaking of the light of day, we read, "The sun rose upon Jacob as he passed Peniel." Jacob could finally say, "I have seen God face to face and yet my life is preserved." (Verse 30)

Jacob Holds on for God's Blessing

Jacob turned to God with the same determination and tenacity he had used on everyone else and he held on for dear life. He held on for a blessing. We are told Jacob prevailed, his life was preserved but he carried the rest of his life the mark of his struggle with God. Jacob had dealt with the terrifying face of the One who is hidden in sovereignty, but who loves us so much he "stoops to our weakness."[5]

His old determination was still there but it seems to have been redirected. He came out of the struggle limping - but with a new name. "I know they call you a trickster," God said, "let me tell you who you really are. Your name is Israel. You are a prince!"

And this is what the good news of God is all about ... that people can change. We find Jacob coming out into the sunlight after his all night struggle with God . . . and saying for the first time, "I have seen God face to face. God's name is still a mystery, but he told me who I am. I am no longer Jacob. I am Israel."

Mr. Edwards had finally "conquered his want-er," he told me. He had given up his desire for more and more "things." But it had not been without struggle and pain.

Mr. Edwards had also been wounded in the struggle before he finally came out into the sunlight. Strangely, it came about in the midst of agony over the terminal illness of his only son who developed leukemia. Mr. Edwards, in the midst of his grief over the death of his son, had seen God. He said, "I found God in the grief and it is enough."

In struggling with God to the place of surrendering our illusions of our own strength and self-sufficiency, we know the power of God's love, forgiveness and amazing grace.

As Mr. Edwards said, as Jacob finally said, and as a little girl said in misquoting Psalm 23, "The Lord is my shepherd, that's all I want." Amen.

Notes
[1] Dr. Gail O'Day. Class lecture at Candler School of Theology, Emory University.

[2] Genesis 25:29-34

[3] Genesis 29:16-17

[4] Walter Brueggemann. *Interpretation Commentary*. Vol 1. p 268-269.

[5] Philippians 2:5-6

Actions Speak Louder Than Words

James 1:17-25

Every good gift and every perfect gift is from above, and comes down from the Father of lights, with whom there is no variation or shadow of turning. On His own will He brought us forth by the word of truth, that we might be a kind of first fruits of His creatures. So then, my beloved brethren, let every man be swift to hear and slow to speak, slow to wrath. For the wrath of man does not produce the righteousness of God. Therefore lay aside all filthiness and overflow of wickedness, and receive with meekness the implanted word, which is able to save your souls. But be doers of the word, and not hearers only, deceiving yourselves. For if anyone is a hearer of the word and not a doer, he is like a man observing his natural face in a mirror. For he observes himself, goes away, and immediately forgets what kind of man he was. Pure and undefiled religion before God and the Father is this: to visit orphans and widows in their trouble, and to keep oneself unspotted from the world.

~James 1:17-25~

Actions Speak Louder Than Words

James 1:17-25

But be doers of the word, and not hearers only, deceiving yourselves.
~James 1:22~

In the Faith Chapter of the Bible, Hebrews 11, faith is described using the nouns "substance" and "evidence." Faith is defined as "the substance of things hoped for and the evidence of things not seen."

In the book of James, faith is also a verb. Faith is something we do (James 1:22).

Christianity is more than a religion or a philosophy. It is a lifestyle...a way of doing ...as well as a way of being. It is based on the heart-changing and life-changing grace that we receive when we accept Jesus Christ as Savior and Lord of our life.

James (James 1:22-27) tells us that the willingness to do what one hears from God...is what characterizes genuine faith. "If we just listen and do not obey, it is like looking at our face in the mirror. As soon as we walk away, we forget what we look like."

Some of us, as we get older, may want to forget what we look like. When I speak to senior citizens' groups I remind them (and me) about one of the laws of compensation. As we age, our eyes get dimmer, so when we look in the mirror we do not always see all our wrinkles and age lines. As Cary Fellman reminds us:

Ode to Myopia

My face in the mirror
Isn't wrinkled or drawn.
My house isn't dirty,
The cobwebs are gone.
My garden looks lovely
And so does my lawn.
I think I will not
Put my glasses back on.

~Cary Fellman~

Some of us may be like Bevel Jones, who spoke at a recent mission event I attended. He said when he looked in the mirror that morning he kept trying to change the channel.

James reminds us to keep looking steadily and clearly into God's law...not to mirror our own finite thoughts... but to get a word from the infinite God.

Walking the Walk and Talking the Talk

I am not a sports fan, but someone called my attention to an article in the *Atlanta Journal* about a fullback with the Atlanta Falcons. His name is Bob and his faith in Christ is worked out in what he does and how he lives. Bob was an eighth grader when his parents invited Christ into their lives. Bob witnessed the dramatic change in their lives, so he became a Christian a few months later.

When Bob was playing in Chicago someone asked about his lifestyle. He knew some might make fun of him when they learned he took seriously the teachings of the Bible and would remain a virgin until he married. Bob, a graduate of Northwestern University with a degree in

Electrical Engineering, decided that if speaking out helped just one youth, it was worth any harassment.

In the article Bob said Christian adults are letting our youth down when they know what is right but are not getting the information out to our young people because it might be politically incorrect by the standards of Hollywood and academia.

We expect our youth to take on our values. At the same time we are not giving them practical reasons for practicing sexual abstinence before marriage in a world of AIDS and sexually transmitted diseases.

We need to give our young people reasons for not drinking. We need to set the example in a world of high powered automobiles and DUIs and a time when one out of ten people who drink become alcoholic almost from the beginning and according to statistics many more become problem drinkers.

If the church does not tell the truth, we can be sure people who have a vested interest in a multibillion dollar alcohol industry will not. So it is good to have successful sports figures, not just talking the talk but walking the walk.

Good Luck, Bad Luck, Who is to Say?

I read a story recently about a poor farmer who had only one horse he depended on for his living.[1] His horse pulled the plow and was his only means of transportation. One day a bee stung the horse and it ran away into the mountains.

His neighbors in the village heard and came by to tell him how sorry they were to hear about his "bad luck" in losing his horse. The old farmer said to his neighbors, "Good luck, bad luck ... who is to say?"

A week later the horse came home and with him were twelve fine wild horses. The old man and his son corralled these fine horses. Again the news of the farmer's windfall spread throughout the village and his neighbors came back to congratulate him on his good luck. Again the old farmer just shrugged and said; "Good luck, bad luck ... who is to say?"

The only son of the farmer was one day trying to tame one of the fine wild horses and the horse threw him off and his leg was broken in three places. When word of the accident spread the villagers came back saying, "We are sorry to hear of the accident and the bad luck of your son getting hurt." The old farmer just shrugged and said, "Good luck, bad luck ... who is to say?"

Two weeks later war broke out between the Provinces. The army came through signing to duty every able-bodied man under sixty. The son did not have to go because of his injury ...which turned out to save his life because every soldier in the village who went was killed in battle.

The old farmer was wise in accepting the fact that we human beings, regardless of advantages or education or money, are not wise enough to make final judgments on what is good luck or bad luck.

Now We See Through a Glass Darkly

The old farmer was profoundly wise in accepting his inability to make a final verdict until all the evidence was in. As Paul tells us, "now we see through a glass darkly."

James wants us to know (James 1:17) that God is the father of lights with whom there is no variation nor shadow of turning. We are wise to remember that we are not in a position to make a final judgment on some things that happen to us. Some events that have every appearance of bad luck . . . in the mysterious unfolding of life . . . may turn out to bring unexpected good.[2]

The Genesis of our Bible teaches this same timeless truth — the truth that the fruit of the tree of knowledge of good and evil is deadly poison for human beings. Genesis teaches that we did not create the universe and therefore we do not have the capacity to determine the ultimate nature of these realities. We may flex our muscles and spout off our learning in the arts and sciences, but I visit in hospitals and nursing homes enough to know . . . we are not always in charge of our own body. The arts and the sciences are constantly being revised and "new scientific truth" is brought forth and yesterday's "old scientific truth" is being discarded.

In one sense, I had the privilege of going through seminary twice. I actually received a PHT (Putting Hubby Through) degree from Emory University in 1958 when my husband earned a Masters of Divinity from Candler School of Theology.

When my husband was a student at Emory, because of my interest and calling, I read most of the books he brought into the house. Rudolf Bultmann was one of the major theologians in the 1950s with his works on form criticism and "demythologizing" the New Testament. Martin Buber, the Jewish thinker, was cited often with his "I and Thou" relationship theology. When I attended the same seminary in the 1980s, neither Bultmann nor Buber was on our reading lists.

The point is: human wisdom and the combined wisdom of noted thinkers often change with the times. We see this illustrated in the medical field . . . in science as well as in theology. We see this idea reflected . . . mirrored in our schools, TV programs and newspapers every day.

Faith is Something We Do

How wonderful to be privileged to gather around the timeless wisdom of the Bible…the word of God that "stands written" with the eternal truth for every generation. This is basically the message of this text in the book of James.

James wants us to know that "faith is something we do." Our actions (our behavior) do indeed speak louder and clearer than our words. The Lord wants to rescue us from our damaging lifestyles and sins because God loves us and wants the best for us.

Therefore, when the Bible states clear and direct and strong moral proclamations about certain behaviors, you do not have to be a religious fanatic or a bigot to take it seriously.

The people who are handing out condoms in public schools in the name of "raging hormones" are giving kids the mistaken idea that hormones do not rage beyond youth so they had better take advantage while they can.

Too often, our youth are advised to sell their future blessings for a mess of porridge . . . like Esau who so devalued his birthright that for immediate gratification, he lost his blessing for a lifetime and lost the blessing that would have gone to his children.

I do not want us to so devalue our birthright as children of God that we sell out to Hollywood, money or political correctness and lose the birthright our fore-parents fought to give us.

James tells us in this lesson from the Bible today that God wants to lead us into whatever changes are needed in our lifestyles . . . even if they are painful in the short run. God wants to lead us into changes that will bring blessedness now and, in the long run, joy for a lifetime and beyond into eternal life.

A Story

One day in 1997 (8/17/97), I turned on the TV to "Christopher Closeup," an interview-type program hosted by a priest. I tuned in just in time to hear a distinguished Ph.D.-type talking to the host. He was telling how he had been invited to speak a few years ago at John Brown University.

He wondered about the origin of the name "John Brown University." He decided it would not likely have been named for the John Brown of "John Brown's body lies a-mouldering in the grave" fame! So he wrote for a brochure and learned the John Brown who founded the university had been a traveling evangelist. As he was preparing to go to the university to give his speech he felt "a little condescending," he said, identifying the term "evangelist" with radical TV evangelists.

On the morning of the speech, his father called from Tennessee and asked about his day and what he was about. So this distinguished speaker mentioned to his dad that he was about to catch a plane to go out west to speak at John Brown University. His dad replied, "Oh yes, I know about that university. It was under John Brown's preaching that my dad was saved."

In relating this story he turned to his host and explained that "saved" is the term commonly used in some church groups for becoming a Christian.

The rest of the story is that this man's grandfather had been from a non-Christian, poor, very disadvantaged family in the hills of Tennessee. At the age of 16 he had struck out on his own.

He happened to encounter John Brown's preaching and became a Christian. When he was ready to get married, he married a Christian girl…and established a Christian home…and thus his life and the life of his family and his descendents were guided by God.

I thought as I heard this story, what better word could be found in all the dictionary than the word "saved" to describe what happens to individuals and even families when Christ comes into a person's life. Not just saved from the "wrath to come" that John Wesley and the early circuit riders preached about, but also saved from illiteracy, ignorance, poverty . . . spiritual poverty and often economic poverty also . . . as we join our disability with God's ability. Christians established the first schools and the first Ivy League colleges in our nation.

Verse 25 in James 1 speaks of looking into the perfect law of God . . . not to mirror our own flawed wisdom but to point us beyond human understanding to the liberating message of mercy and grace. **Amen.**

Notes
[1] John Claypool, *The Library of Distinctive Sermons*, General Editor, Gary W. Kingston. p. 31.

[2] Ibid

Liberty in Law

Exodus 20: 1-17

And God spake all these words saying: I am the Lord your God, who brought you out of the land of Egypt, out of the house of bondage, You shall have no other gods before Me. You shall not make for yourself a carved image - any likeness of anything that is in heaven above, or that is in the earth beneath, or that is in the water under the earth. You shall not bow down to them or serve them. I, the Lord your God, am a jealous God, visiting the iniquity of the fathers upon the children to the third and fourth generation of those who hate me, But showing mercy to thousands who love me and keep my commandments. You shall not take the name of the Lord your God in vain, for the Lord will not hold you guiltless who takes His name in vain. Remember the Sabbath day to keep it holy. Six days you shall labor and do all your work. But the seventh day is the Sabbath of the Lord your God. In it you shall do no work: you, nor your son, nor your daughter, nor your male servant, nor your female servant, nor your cattle, nor your stranger who is in your gates. For in six days the Lord made the heavens and the earth, the sea, and all that is in them, and rested the seventh day. Therefore the Lord blessed the Sabbath day and hallowed it. Honor your father and your mother, that your days may be long upon the land which the Lord God is giving you. You shall not murder. You shall not commit adultery. You shall not steal. You shall not bear false witness against your neighbor. You shall not covet your neighbor's house, you shall not covet your neighbor's wife, nor his male servant, nor his female servant, nor his ox, nor his donkey nor anything that is your neighbor's.

~Exodus 20:1-17~

Liberty in Law

Exodus 20: 1-17

I am the Lord your God who brought you out of the land of Egypt,
out of the house of bondage.
~Exodus: 20:2~

Some of you may remember one of Norman Rockwell's famous paintings on a cover of the *Saturday Evening Post* that shows a woman buying a turkey. The turkey is lying on the scales and the butcher is standing back of the counter with an apron tied around his waist and a pencil behind his ear. Both the woman and the butcher have pleased expressions on their faces as the butcher is pushing down on the scales with his big thumb and the woman is pushing up on the scales with her dainty forefinger and neither is aware of what the other is doing.

Neither the woman nor the butcher would consider themselves a thief. But apparently both of them saw nothing wrong with a little deception that would make a few cents for the butcher and save a few cents for the woman.[1]

This gives us a picture of our human tendency toward self-centeredness and deceit. And here comes God with the Ten Commandments reminding us that there are eternal laws in the universe by which we must live if life is going to come out right.[2]

I was privileged to serve as pastor of the precious East Point Avenue congregation for four years after mandatory retirement. In a Sunday school classroom on my last Sunday there, several members were saying all the nice things one says as a pastor is leaving. One man said, "I will never forget Ruth saying (so-and-so)." This started several others remembering phrases I had used in sermons. Then one woman said, "I will never forget Ruth saying, 'The laws of God were written in our bodies and in our psyches before they were put in The Book.'"

The Ten Commandments are a priceless gift from God because the moral laws of the universe were indeed written in our body and our psyche before they were put in our Book of Faith. Life does not support stealing, will not support murder, will not support adultery, will not support working 24/7. God tells us to take one day a week to stop and take time to rest and worship and remember we are more than what we do!

This is just as true today as when Moses brought these important instructions down from Mt. Sinai. In other words, God's commandments are our directions for life. They are our Manufacturer's instructions straight from our Loving Father. God wants to protect us, just as we who are parents want to protect our children so they can live to enjoy life.

Is Cannibalism Wrong?

I read recently a comment that students, rather than developing moral principles, (in the reporter's words, not mine) merely "develop skills enabling them to rationalize anything short of cannibalism." How many of us think cannibalism is wrong? The fact that most of us believe cannibalism is wrong indicates that we all draw the line somewhere in issues of right and wrong.

So, in our post-modern age when people say there are no absolutes and find it impossible to agree on standards of right and wrong, we are seeing scandals in the business world as well as in our schools. What more and more of us are beginning to realize is that this kind of behavior is the logical result of the moral relativism that permeates our culture. It is so much a part of our daily news that we are all affected.

Human Beings Are Special

No document has influenced the world as much as the Ten Commandments! In our Western civilization, Jews and Christians both Protestant and Catholic, hold the Ten Commandments as principles upon which to build their lives and upon which to build a civilization. Indeed our civil laws of liberty and justice for all are rooted in this covenant law of God on tablets of stone given to Moses at Mount Sinai.

Life With Wings

In recent years atheists in our country have brought suit to remove the plaques and monuments of the Ten Commandments from all government buildings.

The Bible tells us human beings are special! We are all made in the image of God . . . including those accused of crime. Our due process tradition was not begun by the American Civil Liberties Union but by The Bible - "the Book" some have fought to keep out of the hands of school children.

Separation of Church and State

I love the hymn "America the Beautiful" and the second verse that says. "America, America, God mend thine every flaw, Confirm thy soul in self control, thy liberty in Law." The hymn writer knew and God knows that liberty is found in law and not in lawlessness. A God of love gave us these laws. The Ten Commandments are the source of our laws and as such were framed and placed on the walls of courthouses and schools throughout our country.

In recent years, ACLU lawyers have fought against Christian symbols including the public display of the Ten Commandments, saying it violates the principles of the separation of church and state. Not true!

The phrase "separation of church and state" means that the United States is not to have a "state church." England had a state church. The Episcopal Church in England is still the "Church of England." In fact the Queen of England is the titular head of the church as well as the state. The Egyptians never had a code of law. They considered their emperor to be LAW. George Washington was so loved and revered some wanted to make him king after our revolution; but Washington and our founding fathers decided we should not have a king. Not "Rex lex" ("King is law") but "Lex Rex" ("Law is King") . . . and we would also not have a "Church of the United States" but have equality and freedom of religion. Some of them were Deists, but most of our founding fathers were Christians.

Christianity Taught the World to Care

Some of you may remember a time when, after a revival meeting, people would remark, "John got religion last night," meaning he was converted to Christ. In other words, religion in the United States and the West was Christianity. Our liberty was based on the Law of God as given to us in the Christian Bible.

The heritage of the West is like none other the world has ever seen, in spite of its accommodations to the worldwide system of slavery, class and race distinction and "survival of the fittest."

Christianity gave us new concepts of law, government and human rights based on Biblical values. As more and more Christians became literate and learned the New Testament's clear teaching that God is not a respecter of persons, laws against all discrimination were enforced.

Our artists and composers created masterpieces in the sciences, in literature, and art. We see the same story in medicine. For example, Christianity built the first hospitals. The Greek and Roman civilizations were great in many ways but in the whole city of ancient Rome, there was not a single hospital. As Baron Friedrich von Hugel said, "Christianity taught the world to care."

Our founding fathers were wise enough not to want the state running the church, which would make problems for the church as well as the state. But it would have been unthinkable for our founding fathers to take all vestiges of the Christian faith from our schools or government offices. If we do not have laws we become lawless. We are seeing a "law-less-ness" now . . . even in some public schools.

"IN GOD WE TRUST" is on our coins and included in the fourth verse of our National Anthem. Scripture verses are etched in stone at the Jefferson Monument as well as many other historic places in Washington, DC. It is the Christian World View that invites other cultures and religions into America to enjoy our freedoms.

Ten Suggestions

A few years ago, Ted Turner, in criticizing the negativity of the Ten Commandments came forth with his own "Ten Suggestions" and the Atlanta papers gave them a prominent space. When we see our toddler hitting someone with his little hand and little strength, we might just suggest "no - no, honey." But when we see him running toward a hot stove, or running toward the road or some real or potential danger, we dash out and command that he stop.

I have used a computer to do a mountainous amount of typing for many years. I have found I have to follow certain instructions from the maker of the computer. If I ever decided I knew more than the maker of the computer knows, I would be in serious trouble. In fact it is interesting that the computer is set up by commands, not suggestions.

We have to follow the instructions of the maker, and the more we follow, the better it works and the more awesome it is. In fact, it does not take long to realize one had better follow the commands or it will not work.

God's Law is the Gift of His Love

Some people seem to think God roams the world looking for people who may be having a good time so He can zap them. No! God's law is the gift of His love for our joy. It is in God's law that we are given freedom and liberty. God's rules for our life are not arbitrary because God knows that without rules we cannot successfully play the game of life!

My grandson, Dow, visited me one day when he was about seven. When Dow came in he said, "Well, Grandmother, what are we going to do today?" I asked, "What would you like to do?" He replied, "Let's play *Clue*." I said, "All right ... if you will teach me the rules." I learned how to play the game of *Clue* and we had a good time.

We have rules for games ... rules for the road ... traffic laws. Otherwise there would be chaos; and there is chaos if we do not obey the rules. Even to play a game of checkers we must have rules, directions and laws. We do not just move the pieces here and there without rules. If so, it is like babies throwing things in every direction, making a mess to be cleaned up.

What an analogy of people trying to live without rules! We do not break the laws of God – they stand as written. We only break ourselves if we ignore them.

The activists in Hollywood and other enemies of righteousness have managed to convince some of our people that "religion" is a "private matter," that people who witness outside the church are "fanatic and intolerant." Not true. If our fore-parents had kept their faith a private matter, we would never have had the "Protestant work ethic" and the progress and prosperity we have enjoyed in this country.

Reinventing the Wheel of Morality

We do not have to reinvent the wheel of morality. Yet we have people expecting our teenagers to go out into the world to make up their own rules for life as they go along. No direction … no absolutes. As a result, many are messing up their lives with alcohol, other drugs and sexual experimentation because they are expected to live without direction. They are expected to experiment, to invent, to imagine and re-imagine and to decide through trial and error down one road and then another when a God of love has already written out clear directions for a way for life that works.

This belief in one God sets the Israelites apart from other ancient religions. Before God gave this first commandment, He identified Himself, "I am the Lord your God who brought you out of the land of Egypt, out of the house of bondage."

The basis of this commandment is …we are told that "the Lord our God is a jealous God." This statement used to puzzle me because I tend to connect jealousy with envy, pettiness. But "jealous" in this passage comes from the Greek word that means "emotional"; and it means that

God cares so much He is emotional about us. God cares about us. God is not indifferent to what we do and how we live.

Indifference is the Opposite of Love

A man complained to me about his wife getting upset when he "took a drink," but he said she didn't seem to mind at all if other people drank alcoholic beverages. How many of you understand this wife?

Love is emotional. We have concern about those we love ... not only concern about what they do but who they are! There is a fine line here. That is why couples have such a hard time understanding one another. But the marriage is not in trouble when we fight as much as when we become indifferent to one another.

The God who brought the Hebrews out of slavery wanted to keep them - and wants to keep us - out of an even greater bondage. He simplified the rules of life down to ten...one for each finger.

- No other gods.
- No idols.
- God's name is important. We are to bless, not curse.
- For our own sake, we are to stop working one day a week and remember we are more than our possessions or what we do.
- Honor our parents. They are our roots.
- Don't murder, life is precious.
- We are not to play around with our marriage vows. Keeping our covenant with one person is our best chance of growing up.
- If we take what belongs to another, we are the loser.
- Speak the truth. When we twist our word, we limp through life.[3]

The Tenth Commandment

The Tenth Commandment telling us not to "covet" comes silently after the booming "Thou shall nots" about lying, stealing, adultery and murder.

Our community was shocked - in fact it made news all over Georgia and beyond - in July of 2004 when a respected youth leader in a church in Rome was accused of the murder of a fellow church leader. We were later dumbfounded when it was alleged the murdered man's wife was in an affair with the alleged murderer and was an accomplice in planning the murder.

Probably none of us were more shocked than this man and woman who were convicted for murder in 2010. When we begin the hidden sin of coveting, we never know how far down the slippery slope it will take us.

It seems so harmless when we first engage in a flirtation that might lead to adultery. It seems so harmless when we first engage in perhaps soft core pornography that requires more and more explicit materials and often leads to acting out, according to statistics.

These "little" offenses are only revealed when an overt action like adultery or murder brings it into the limelight. Jesus tells us sin begins in the heart with hidden lust and anger.[4]

To covet is dangerous because it is silent and hidden. We do not see "covet." There are no civil laws against covetousness. It is even hard to pronounce so we do not denounce it. Yet this tenth commandment about covetousness covers the other nine. Covetousness is deceptive and goes hand in hand with discontentment, lies, lust and hate. We are not to "covet anything that belongs to someone else... house, spouse, nor anything that belongs to our neighbor."[5]

The awesome message of these commandments is that a God of love has given us guidelines for a successful life as well as given guidelines for what it means to be a civil and liberated human being as well as what it means to be a covenant person and a follower of Jesus Christ.

I have found God's laws to be the liberating directions on the road of life. Someone has said, "When in doubt read the directions." God's directions in the form of the Ten Commandments[6] are the gift of God's boundless love and amazing Grace for our liberty and fulfillment in Jesus. **Amen!**

Notes

[1] Cecil Myers, *Thunder on the Mountain.* p 119-20

[2] Maxie Dunham. *Communicators Commentary.* Lloyd Oglivie, Exodus. p.252.

[3] Barbara Brown Taylor. *Gospel Medicine.* p 57

[4] Matthew 5:22-27

[5] Exodus 20:17

[6] Exodus 20:1-17

In Token and Pledge

Genesis 15: 1-12, 17, 18a

After these things the word of the Lord came to Abram in a vision, saying, "Do not be afraid, Abram, I am your shield, your exceedingly great reward." But Abram said, "Lord God, what will you give me, seeing I go childless, and the heir of my house is Eliezer of Damascus?" Then Abram said, "You have given me no offspring; indeed one born in my house is my heir!" And behold, the word of the Lord came to him saying, "This one shall not be your heir, but one who will come from your own body shall be your heir." Then He brought him outside and said, "Look now toward heaven, and count the stars if you are able to number them." And He said to him, "So shall your descendents be." And Abram believed in the Lord, and He accounted it to him for righteousness. Then God said to Abram, "I am the Lord, who brought you out of Ur of the Chaldeans, to give you this land to inherit it." And Abram said, "Lord God, how shall I know that I will inherit it?" So God said to him, "Bring me a three-year-old heifer, a three-year-old female goat, a three-year-old ram, a turtle dove, and a young pigeon." Then Abram brought all these to Him and cut them in two, down the middle, and placed each piece opposite the other, but he did not cut the birds in two, And when the vultures came down on the carcasses, Abram drove them away. Now when the sun was going down, a deep sleep fell upon Abram. And it came to pass, when the sun went down and it was dark, that behold, there appeared a smoking oven and a burning torch that passed between the pieces. On that same day the Lord made a covenant with Abram.

~Genesis 15:1-12, 17, 18~

In Token and Pledge

Genesis 15: 1-12, 17, 18a

And on that day the Lord made a covenant with Abram.
~Genesis 15:18a~.

The great central theme of our Bible, both the Old and the New Testament, is that of God's covenant relationship with humanity.

The Bible is not our search - not humanity's search - for God, but God's revelation of love for us. After generations of dealing with rebellious people, in the Genesis of the Bible, book one, chapter 12, we see God unfolding his wonderful plan and purpose for all people, beginning with Abraham and Sarah. God calls Abraham to leave his home in Ur of the Chaldes and to travel to a distant but unspecified new land. Abraham responded in faith and obeyed with nothing to cling to but the promises of God. For Abraham it was the long view. There was not much in it immediately for Abraham.

Looking back over my life, I see so often where God took the long view. The genealogists in the Bible take the long view with all the begats that we tend to skip over. I re-read Matthew and noted in the family tree of Jesus, more than half the names we know nothing about and some, like Rahab and Bathsheba, we would just as soon not know about. Yet we see that even in the lineage of Jesus, God sometime uses human weaknesses to magnify Divine power!

One of my daughters, Janice, has published a book entitled *A Different Kind of Strength* about the five women in the genealogy of Jesus and about how God used these women in spite of their failures in God's own time.[1]

Most of us have a problem with this. Ours is a "now" generation. We are into television dramas where a family crisis can be solved in 30 minutes and motion picture detectives can have justice roll down like waters in an hour. We do not like to wait. We want results immediately.

But in Genesis 15, we see Abraham, who set out on his journey of faith in chapter 12, still daring to believe God's promise for the impossible in God's own time.

In the 15th chapter of Genesis he was just plain Abram. We have to get down two chapters later before God changes his name to Abraham and changes Sarai to Sarah.

Abraham believed God's promise about an heir being born to Sarah, and he kept believing when all the evidence was to the contrary. Most of us would have been cynical by now. We would have long since said, "This faith stuff is not working for me."

For several years when our children were young we took a week each summer for a camping trip. As a mother, I think one of the most difficult things about rearing children is riding with them in an automobile! You are on a four or five hour trip and every few minutes one of them will ask the question, "How much longer will it be before we get there?"

I heard about one little boy who was on a family vacation and kept asking this question and finally the father said, "Don't ask me anymore. I'm tired of the question - please keep quiet about it." The little boy got very quiet...then after a while he said in a small whisper, "Daddy, will I still be alive when we get there?"

Abraham must have wondered... "Will I live long enough to see God's promise fulfilled?"

So chapter 15 in the Genesis of our Bible begins with God reassuring fearful old Abraham that he and Sarah will have a son. In spite of the evidence to the contrary, God tells Abraham his descendents will be as numerous as the stars he sees on a clear night!

The Meaning of Faith

Verse 6 tells us, Abraham "believed God and it was accounted to him for righteousness." This keynote comment defines the meaning of faith as implicit trust in God's character - trust in God's promise - even when proof is lacking. This basic attitude of trust is an inner attitude which puts a person in a right relationship with God. This is what righteousness means — "a right relationship with God."

In a very real sense, Abraham had repented as each one of us must do if we are to be saved. Abraham had given up seeing reality as only something he can see and touch and manage.

In a very real sense, this is the Old Testament form of the New Testament doctrine of "Justification by Faith." The tremendous power of faith in God to transform a life is suggested here in Genesis, the first book of the Bible and is underlined in the New Testament by Paul.

This has been the keynote for John Wesley and a host of other Christian leaders throughout the ages; that we do not have to conform to the world; we can be transformed by Jesus Christ. We do not have to follow the crowd. We can maintain a minority view! [2]

"His faith is not grounded in the old flesh of Sarah nor the tired bones of Abraham but in the word of Almighty God." [3]

In Old Testament language...a covenant is cut...not spoken. We see Abram cut the larger animals in half and clear a path. This passing between the broken pieces of the animals symbolized the idea that within the very bodies of the slain animals, the parties of the covenant are united as one. This was their pledge to each other . . . by passing through the severed bodies of the animals, each party said, "May the same thing happen to me . . . may I be torn in half if I do not keep my word." It is like we sometimes said as children, "Cross my heart and hope to die."

Our ceremonies and pledges and covenants today seem colorless compared to this covenant Abraham made with God that dark night. We walk down carpeted aisle, kneel on a padded altar and repeat, "I accept Jesus Christ as my Savior and Lord." Or we stand in a comfortable courthouse and say, "I promise to tell the truth, the whole truth and nothing but the truth, so help me God." Or we stand with our beloved before a minister in an air conditioned sanctuary and repeat, "In token and pledge of the vow and covenant between us made, with this ring I thee wed."

Abraham did all he was told to do and walked, not down a carpeted church aisle, as some of us have too much pride to do, but he walked the bloody path between the animals to make his covenant with God. He even had to guard his part of the bargain by waving off the vultures that came down to eat the carcasses. After all the activity Abraham fell into a fitful sleep.

God's Part of the Covenant

In the midst of such a sleep, Abraham saw a pot of fire and a flaming torch pass between the halves of the slain animals. Abraham saw and he knew it was the Lord God - keeping his part of the covenant.

Do you get the picture? The God of creation walking the bloody path between the severed animals! I vividly remember the first time I really studied this passage of scripture. I could not hold back the tears.

I read this text with great emotion because here we see a God of love, as Paul paints for us in the beautiful poem in Philippians of Jesus "emptying himself of his divinity" and stooping down to make himself available for covenant with any man or woman.[4]

This is the best good news I know! God loves us. God knows, and if we live long enough we will know, we will need more than just a few religious Band-Aids to patch up our brokenness. No ritual "first aid" treatment can heal the grief-bruised and sin-sick soul. We need God for the challenges of life. Our best resources and finest minds are not adequate. We need God.

I heard a young preacher tell the story of when his wife became pregnant with their first child. He said it was an unplanned pregnancy. He was a graduate student and his wife was working and they needed her salary. But even so, when the pregnancy was confirmed they were excited about the baby and accepted congratulations from family and friends.

Then a few days later, his wife began to have a threatened miscarriage and her doctor said it was probably nature's way of terminating a pregnancy where the baby was defective. The husband called a doctor friend who listened to the symptoms and concurred with the first diagnosis and consoled the young man that they could still have more children.

The husband came back and told his wife what the doctor friend had said. He said his wife did not reply and looked at him as if she did not hear him. He said his nerves were about shot. He raised his voice and told her that perhaps they should be grateful because the baby could have been horribly handicapped and led a sad life and they could have more children.

He said he could not believe the horrified look on his wife's face as she screamed, "You don't understand how much I have come to love this baby in the 48 hours I have known of its existence. I want this baby - even if I have to spend the rest of my life taking care of it."

God is Love

God loves us in a strange and wonderful way. What Jesus did for us reveals a Love that is awesome - in spite of our handicap of brokenness and sin. God seems to have forgotten His own dignity and place and has given Himself to deal lovingly in covenant with us. The same God who came down to Abraham and walked between the animals and, in effect, said, "cross my heart and hope to die," in Jesus Christ He hung on a bloody cross to get to us and save us. He stretched out His arms on a cross and said, "This is how much I love you!" **Amen**.

Notes
[1] Janice Shaw Crouse, *A Different Kind of Strength*

[2] Walter Brueggemann, *Interpretation Commentary.* Vol. 1, p.141

[3] Ibid

[4] Philippians 2:6-9

About The Author

Ruth Shaw holds a Master of Divinity degree from Candler School of Theology, Emory University. She also earned a bachelor's degree in Interdisciplinary Studies from the College of Arts and Sciences at Georgia State University and a Certificate in Gerontology for work in the field of aging.

In recent years, in addition to serving as pastor at Rico United Methodist Church in Palmetto, Grantville First United Methodist Church and

East Point Avenue United Methodist Church in East Point, Ruth has read her poetry and spoken on the subject of aging to many church and civic groups. She also enjoys cooking, and often cooks for 25 to 50 family members and friends at Thanksgiving and other special occasions.

Since retiring to Rome in 1998, Ruth has served on the staff at Trinity United Methodist Church for 4 years, as a short term interim pastor at Lyerly United Methodist Church for five months, at Oostanaula United Methodist Church for 13 months and with Livingston United Methodist for 12 months.

Ruth Baird Shaw is the widow of the Reverend Charles C. Shaw who was an elder in the North Georgia Conference of the United Methodist Church and served from 1954 until his death on December 3, 1986.

Children of Charles and Ruth Shaw

Janice Shaw Crouse, married to Gilbert Crouse
Joan Shaw Turrentine, married to Jim Turrentine
Charles Terrell Shaw, married to Sheila Matthews Shaw
Carol Shaw Johnston, married to Ron Johnston
Deborah Shaw Lewis, married to Gregg Lewis
Beth Shaw Roszel, married to Chuck Roszel
David Baird Shaw, married to Vicki Brown Shaw

Grandchildren of Charles and Ruth Shaw

Lyn Turrentine Davis
Charmaine Crouse Yoest
Gilbert Crouse, Jr.
Steven Turrentine
Larisa Johnston Hensiek
Joseph (Joey) Johnston
Andrew Lewis
Joshua Hearn
Matthew Lewis
Amanda Hearn Sims
Brannon Shaw
Lisette Lewis
Jessica Shaw Rogers
Benjamin Lewis
Lillian Shaw
Jonathan Lewis
Catherine (Katie) Shaw
Haley Shaw

Great-Grandchildren of Charles and Ruth Shaw

Rachael Turrentine
Hannah Yoest
Dow Turrentine
John Yoest
Lewis Crouse
Helena (Gibby) Yoest
Mark Crouse
Brianne Davis
AnnaGrace Turrentine
Natalie Davis
Sarah Yoest
Ethan Davis
Lillian (Lily) Hensiek
Sophia (Sophie) Hensiek
James Yoest
Emma Hearn
Evelyn (Evey) Johnston
Alexander (Alex) Rogers

Printed in Great Britain
by Amazon

61837784R00077